CLASSIC
FILM
SCRIPTS

THE CABINET OF
Dr. CALIGARI

a film by

Robert Wiene
Carl Mayer and Hans Janowitz

English translation and description of action
by R. V. Adkinson

Lorrimer Publishing

Publisher and Editor: Andrew Sinclair

ISBN paper 0 85647 084 8

Distributed exclusively in the United States of America, its territories, possessions, protectorates, mandated territories, the Philippines and the Dominion of Canada by Frederick Ungar Publishing Company Inc., 36 Cooper Square, New York, N.Y. 10003

Distributed exclusively in the United Kingdom and Commonwealth by Lorrimer (Sales) Limited
Inquiries should be addressed to Lorrimer Publishing Limited, 16 Tite Street, London SW3 4HZ.

Cover design: Fred Price

British Library Cataloguing in Publication Data

Wiene, Robert
    The cabinet of Dr Caligari
    I. Title   II. Mayer, Carl   III. Janowitz, Hans
    791.43'72   PN1997

ISBN 0-85647-084-8

CONTENTS

FOREWORD

by Andrew Sinclair

The Cabinet of Dr. Caligari has again proved its prophetic powers. In Russia, dissidents are no longer subjected to the camps of the Gulag; they are put into mental hospitals until they conform to the power of the state and to its image of Soviet society. Their minds are changed by drugs, confinement and psychiatric techniques, not by hypnosis; but as in the asylum of Dr. Caligari, the dissidents are mixed with the insane, as if protest or perception of the truth were another form of madness.

Wiene's film changed the authors' revolutionary demonstration of the madness of authority into approval of authority confining those who thought it mad. So in Russia and some other dictatorial countries, the ideology of the party calls insane all those who disagree with it. And those who are instructed in that ideology under that hypnosis now called brainwashing may be sent, like Cesare, to kill and be killed in the service of the power of the state.

Wiene's film prophesied not only the rise of Hitler and the dementia of Nazi beliefs in Germany, but also the abuse of psychiatry in the service of the totalitarian state.

Dr. Caligari lives.

Acknowledgements and thanks are due to the National Film Archive for loaning a print of the film; Herman Weinberg and the Museum of Modern Art for supplying stills. 'Caligari' by Siegfried Kracauer is taken from *From Caligari to Hitler* by Siegfried Kracauer and reprinted by permission of the publishers, Princeton University Press. 'Carl Mayer's Debut' by Erich Pommer and 'Carl Mayer—An Appreciation' by Paul Rotha are taken from *The Film Till Now* and reprinted by permission of the publishers, Vision Press.

CALIGARI

by Siegfried Kracauer

The Czech Hans Janowitz, one of the two authors of the film *Das Cabinet des Dr. Caligari* (*The Cabinet of Dr. Caligari*), was brought up in Prague — that city where reality fuses with dreams, and dreams turn into visions of horror.[1] One evening in October 1913 this young poet was strolling through a fair at Hamburg, trying to find a girl whose beauty and manner had attracted him. The tents of the fair covered the Reeperbahn, known to any sailor as one of the world's chief pleasure spots. Nearby, on the Holstenwall, Lederer's gigantic Bismark monument stood sentinel over the ships in the harbour. In search of the girl, Janowitz followed the fragile trail of a laugh which he thought hers into a dim park bordering the Holstenwall. The laugh, which apparently served to lure a young man, vanished somewhere in the shrubbery. When, a short time later, the young man departed, another shadow, hidden until then in the bushes, suddenly emerged and moved along — as if on the scent of that laugh. Passing this uncanny shadow, Janowitz caught a glimpse of him: he looked like an average bourgeois. Darkness reabsorbed the man and made further pursuit impossible. The following day big headlines in the local press announced: 'Horrible sex crime on the Holstenwall! Young Gertrude . . . murdered.' An obscure feeling that Gertrude might have been the girl of the fair impelled Janowitz to attend the victim's funeral. During the ceremony he suddenly had the sensation of discovering the murderer, who had not yet been captured. The man he suspected seemed to recognise him, too. It was the bourgeois — the shadow in the bushes.

---

[1] The following episode, along with other data appearing in my pages on *Caligari*, is drawn from an interesting manuscript Mr. Hans Janowitz has written about the genesis of this film. I feel greatly indebted to him for having put his material at my disposal. I am thus in a position to base my interpretation of *Caligari* on the true inside story, up to now unknown.

Carl Mayer, co-author with Janowitz of *Caligari*, was born in the Austrian provincial capital of Graz, where his father, a wealthy businessman, would have prospered had he not been obsessed by the idea of becoming a ' scientific ' gambler. In the prime of life he sold his property, went, armed with an infallible ' system ', to Monte Carlo, and reappeared a few months later in Graz, broke. Under the stress of this catastrophe, the monomaniac father turned the sixteen-year-old Carl and his three younger brothers out into the street and finally committed suicide. A mere boy, Carl Mayer was responsible for the three children. While he toured through Austria, peddling barometers, singing in choirs and playing extras in peasant theatres, he became increasingly interested in the stage. There was no branch of theatrical production which he did not explore during those years of nomadic life — years full of experiences that were to be of immense use in his future career as a film poet. At the beginning of the war, the adolescent made his living by sketching Hindenburg portraits on post cards in Munich cafés. Later in the war, Janowitz reports, he had to undergo repeated examinations of his mental condition. Mayer seems to have been very embittered against the high-ranking military psychiatrist in charge of his case.

The war was over. Janowitz, who from its outbreak had been an officer in an infantry regiment, returned as a convinced pacifist, animated by hatred of an authority which had sent millions of men to death. He felt that absolute authority was bad in itself. He settled in Berlin, met Carl Mayer there, and soon found out that this eccentric young man, who had never before written a line, shared his revolutionary moods and views. Why not express them on the screen? Intoxicated with Wegener's films, Janowitz believed that this new medium might lend itself to powerful poetic revelations. As youth will, the two friends embarked on endless discussions that hovered around Janowitz' Holstenwall adventure as well as Mayer's mental duel with the psychiatrist. These stories seemed to evoke and supplement each other. After such discussions the pair would stroll through the night, irresistibly attracted by a dazzling and clamorous fair on Kantstrasse. It was a bright jungle, more hell than paradise, but a paradise to those who had exchanged the horror of war for the terror of want. One evening, Mayer dragged his companion to a side show by which he had been impressed. Under the title ' Man and Machine ' it presented a strong man who achieved miracles of strength in an apparent stupor. He acted as if he were hypnotised. The strangest thing was that he accompanied his feats with utterances which affected the spellbound spectators as pregnant forebodings.

Any creative process approaches a moment when only one additional experience is needed to integrate all elements into a whole. The mysterious figure of the strong man supplied such an experience. On the night of this show the friends first visualised the original story of *Caligari*. They wrote the manuscript in the following six weeks. Defining the part each took in the work, Janowitz calls himself ' the father who planted the seed and Mayer the mother who conceived and ripened it.' At the end, one small problem arose : the authors were at a loss as to what to christen their main character, a psychiatrist shaped after Mayer's archenemy during the war. A rare volume, *Unknown Letters of Stendhal,* offered the solution. While Janowitz was skimming through this find of his, he happened to notice that Stendhal, just come from the battlefield, met at La Scala in Milan an officer named Caligari. The name clicked with both authors.

Their story is located in a fictitious North German town near the Dutch border, significantly called Holstenwall. One day a fair moves into the town, with merry-go-rounds and side shows — among the latter that of Dr. Caligari, a weird, bespectacled man advertising the somnambulist Cesare. To procure a license, Caligari goes to the town hall, where he is treated haughtily by an arrogant official. The following morning this official is found murdered in his room, which does not prevent the townspeople from enjoying the fair's pleasures. Along with numerous onlookers, Francis and Alan — two students in love with Jane, a medical man's daughter — enter the tent of Dr. Caligari and watch Cesare slowly stepping out of an upright, coffinlike box. Caligari tells the thrilled audience that the somnambulist will answer questions about the future. Alan, in an excited state, asks how long he has to live. Cesare opens his mouth; he seems to be dominated by a terrific, hypnotic power

7

emanating from his master. 'Until dawn,' he answers. At dawn Francis learns that his friend has been stabbed in exactly the same manner as the official. The student, suspicious of Caligari, persuades Jane's father to assist him in an investigation. With a search warrant the two force their way into the showman's wagon and demand that he end the trance of his medium. However, at this very moment they are called away to the police station to attend the examination of a criminal who has been caught in the act of killing a woman, and who now frantically denies that he is the pursued serial murderer.

Francis continues spying on Caligari and, after nightfall, secretly peers through a window of the wagon. But while he imagines he sees Cesare lying in his box, Cesare in reality breaks into Jane's bedroom, lifts a dagger to pierce the sleeping girl, gazes at her, puts the dagger away and flees, with the screaming Jane in his arms, over roofs and roads. Chased by her father, he drops the girl, who is then escorted home, whereas the lonely kidnapper dies of exhaustion. As Jane, in flagrant contradiction of what Francis believes to be the truth, insists on having recognised Cesare, Francis approaches Caligari a second time to solve the torturing riddle. The two policemen in his company seize the coffinlike box, and Francis draws out of it — a dummy representing the somnambulist. Profiting by the investigators' carelessness, Caligari himself manages to escape. He seeks shelter in a lunatic asylum. The student follows him, calls on the director of the asylum to inquire about the fugitive, and recoils horror-struck: the director and Caligari are one and the same person.

The following night — the director has fallen asleep — Francis and three members of the medical staff whom he has initiated into the case search the director's office and discover material fully establishing the guilt of this authority in psychiatric matters. Among a pile of books they find an old volume about a showman named Caligari who, in the eighteenth century, travelled through North Italy, hypnotised his medium Cesare into murdering sundry people, and, during Cesare's absence, substituted a wax figure to deceive the police. The main exhibit is the director's clinical records; they show evidence that he desired to verify the account of Caligari's hypnotic faculties, that his desire grew into an obsession, and that, when a somnambulist was entrusted to his care, he could not resist the temptation of repeating with him those terrible games. He had adopted the identity of Caligari. To make him admit his crimes, Francis confronts the director with the corpse of his tool, the somnambulist. No sooner does the monster realise Cesare is dead than he begins to rave. Trained attendants put him into a strait jacket.

This horror tale in the spirit of E. T. A. Hoffmann was an outspoken revolutionary story. In it, as Janowitz indicates, he and Carl Mayer half intentionally stigmatised the omnipotence of a state authority manifesting itself in universal conscription and declarations of war. The German war government seemed to the authors the prototype of such voracious authority. Subjects of the Austro-Hungarian monarchy, they were in a better position than most citizens of the Reich to penetrate the fatal tendencies inherent in the German system. The character of Caligari embodies these tendencies; he stands for an unlimited authority that idolises power as such and, to satisfy its lust for domination, ruthlessly violates all human rights and values. Functioning as a mere instrument, Cesare is not so much a guilty murderer as Caligari's innocent victim. This is how the authors themselves understood him. According to the pacifist-minded Janowitz, they had created Cesare with the dim design of portraying the common man who, under the pressure of compulsory military service, is drilled to kill and to be killed. The revolutionary meaning of the story reveals itself unmistakably at the end, with the disclosure of the psychiatrist as Caligari: reason overpowers unreasonable power, insane authority is symbolically abolished. Similar ideas were also being expressed on the contemporary stage, but the authors of *Caligari* transferred them to the screen without including any of those eulogies of the authority-freed ' New Man ' in which many expressionist plays indulged.

A miracle occurred: Erich Pommer, chief executive of Decla-Bioscop, accepted this unusual, if not subversive, script. Was it a miracle? Since, in those early postwar days the conviction prevailed that foreign markets could only be conquered by artistic achievements, the German film industry was of course anxious to experiment in the field of aesthetically qualified entertainment.[2] Art assured export, and export meant salvation. An ardent partisan of this doctrine, Pommer had moreover an incomparable flair for cinematic values and popular demands. Regardless of whether he grasped the significance of the strange story Mayer and Janowitz submitted to him, he certainly sensed its timely atmosphere and interesting scenic potentialities. He was a born promoter who handled screen and business affairs with equal facility and, above all, excelled in stimulating the creative energies of directors and players. In 1923, Ufa was to make him chief of its entire production.[3] His behind-the-scenes activities were to leave their imprint on the pre-Hitler screen.

Pommer assigned Fritz Lang to direct *Caligari,* but in the middle of the preliminary discussions Lang was ordered to finish his serial *The Spiders;* the distributors of this film urged its completion.[4] Lang's successor was Dr. Robert Wiene. Since his father, a once famous Dresden actor, had become slightly insane towards the end of his life, Wiene was not entirely unprepared to tackle the case of Dr. Caligari. He suggested, in complete harmony with what Lang had planned, an essential change of the original story — a change against which the two authors violently protested. But no one heeded them.[5]

The original story was an account of real horrors; Wiene's version transforms that account into a chimera concocted and narrated by the mentally deranged Francis. To effect this transformation the body of the original story is put into a framing story which introduces Francis as a madman. The film *Caligari* opens with the first of the two episodes composing the frame. Francis is shown sitting on a bench in the park of the lunatic asylum, listening to the confused babble of a fellow sufferer. Moving slowly, like an apparition, a female inmate of the asylum passes by : it is Jane. Francis says to his companion, ' What she and I have experienced is yet more

[2] Vincent, *Histoire de l'Art Cinématographique,* p 140.

[3] *Jahrbuch der Filmindustrie,* 1922–23, pp 35, 46. For an appraisal of Pommer, see Lejeune, *Cinema,* pp 125–31.

[4] Information offered by Mr. Lang.

[5] Extracted from Mr. Janowitz' manuscript. See also Vincent, *Histoire de l'Art Cinématographique,* pp 140, 143–44.

remarkable than the story you have told me. I will tell you. . . . "[6]
Fade-out. Then a view of Holstenwall fades in, and the original
story unfolds, ending, as has been seen, with the identification of
Caligari. After a new fade-out the second and final episode of the
framing story begins. Francis, having finished the narration, follows
his companion back to the asylum, where he mingles with a crowd
of sad figures — among them Cesare, who absent-mindedly caresses
a little flower. The director of the asylum, a mild and understand-
ing-looking person, joins the crowd. Lost in the maze of his hallu-
cinations, Francis takes the director for the nightmarish character
he himself has created and accuses this imaginary fiend of being a
dangerous madman. He screams, he fights the attendants in a
frenzy. The scene is switched over to a sickroom, with the director
putting on horn-rimmed spectacles which immediately change his
appearance: it seems to be Caligari who examines the exhausted
Francis. After this, he removes his spectacles and, *all mildness,*
tells his assistants that Francis believes him to be Caligari. Now that
he understands the case of his patient, the director concludes, he
will be able to heal him. With this cheerful message the audience is
dismissed.

Janowitz and Mayer knew why they raged against the framing
story: it perverted, if not reversed, their intrinsic intentions. While
the original story exposed the madness inherent in authority,
Wiene's *Caligari* glorified authority and convicted its antagonist
of madness. A revolutionary film was thus turned into a conformist
one — following the much-used pattern of declaring some normal
but troublesome individual insane and sending him to a lunatic
asylum. This change undoubtedly resulted not so much from
Wiene's personal predilections as from his instinctive submission to
the necessities of the screen; films, at least commercial films, are
forced to answer to mass desires. In its changed form *Caligari*
was no longer a product expressing, at best, sentiments charac-
teristic of the intelligentsia, but a film supposed equally to be in
harmony with what the less educated felt and liked.

If it holds true that during the postwar years most Germans

---

[6] Film license, issued by Board of Censors, Berlin, 1921 and 1925 (Museum of
Modern Art Library, clipping files); *Film Society Programme,* March 14, 1926.

11

eagerly tended to withdraw from a harsh outer world into the intangible realm of the soul, Wiene's version was certainly more consistent with their attitude than the original story; for, by putting the original into a box, this version faithfully mirrored the general retreat into a shell. In *Caligari* (and several other films of the time) the device of a framing story was not only an aesthetic form, but also had symbolic content. Significantly, Wiene avoided mutilating the original story itself. Even though *Caligari* had become a conformist film, it preserved and emphasised this revolutionary story — as a madman's fantasy. Caligari's defeat now belonged among psychological experiences. In this way Wiene's film does suggest that during their retreat into themselves the Germans were stirred to reconsider their traditional belief in authority. Down to the bulk of Social Democratic workers they refrained from revolutionary action; yet at the same time a psychological revolution seems to have prepared itself in the depths of the collective soul. The film reflects this double aspect of German life by coupling a reality in which Caligari's authority triumphs with a hallucination in which the same authority is overthrown. There could be no better configuration of symbols for that uprising against the authoritarian dispositions which apparently occurred under the cover of a behaviour-rejecting uprising.

Janowitz suggested that the settings for *Caligari* be designed by the painter and illustrator Alfred Kubin, who, a forerunner of the surrealists, made eerie phantoms invade harmless sceneries and visions of torture emerge from the subconscious. Wiene took to the idea of painted canvases, but preferred to Kubin three expressionist artists : Hermann Warm, Walter Röhrig and Walter Reimann. They were affiliated with the Berlin Sturm group, which, through Herwarth Walden's magazine *Sturm*, promoted expressionism in every field of art.[7]

Although expressionist painting and literature had evolved years before the war, they acquired a public only after 1918. In this respect the case of Germany somewhat resembled that of Soviet Russia, where, during the short period of war communism, diverse

---

[7] Mr. Janowitz' manuscript; Vincent, *Histoire de l'Art Cinématographique*, p 144; Rotha, *Film Till Now*, p 43.

currents of abstract art enjoyed a veritable heyday.[8] To a revolutionised people expressionism seemed to combine the denial of bourgeois traditions with faith in man's power freely to shape society and nature. On account of such virtues it may have cast a spell over many Germans upset by the breakdown of their universe.[9]

'Films must be drawings brought to life'; this was Hermann Warm's formula at the time that he and his two fellow designers were constructing the *Caligari* world.[10] In accordance with his beliefs, the canvases and draperies of *Caligari* abounded in complexes of jagged, sharp-pointed forms strongly reminiscent of Gothic patterns. Products of a style which by then had become almost a mannerism, these complexes suggested houses, walls, landscapes. Except for a few slips or concessions — some backgrounds opposed the pictorial convention in too direct a manner, while others all but preserved them — the settings amounted to a perfect transformation of material objects into emotional ornaments. With its oblique chimneys on pell-mell roofs, its windows in the form of arrows or kites and its treelike arabesques that were threats rather than trees, Holstenwall resembled those visions of unheard-of cities which the painter Lionel Feininger evoked through his edgy, crys-

---

[8] Kurtz, *Expressionismus,* p 61.

[9] In Berlin, immediately after the war, Karl Heinz Martin staged two little dramas by Ernst Toller and Walter Hasenclever within expressionist settings. Cf Kurtz, *ibid,* p 43; Vincent, *Histoire de l'Art Cinématographique,* pp 142–43; Schapiro, 'Nature of Abstract Art,' *Marxist Quarterly,* January-March 1937, p 97.

[10] Quotation from Kurtz, *Expressionismus,* p 66. Warm's views, which implied a verdict on films as photographed reality, harmonised with those of Viking Eggeling, an abstract Swedish painter living in Germany. Having eliminated all objects from his canvases, Eggeling deemed it logical to involve the surviving geometrical compositions in rhythmic movements. He and his painter friend Hans Richter submitted this idea to Ufa, and Ufa, guided as ever by the maxim that art is good business or, at least, good propaganda, enabled the two artists to go ahead with their experiments. The first abstract films appeared in 1921. While Eggeling — he died in 1925 — orchestrated spiral lines and comb-like figures in a short he called *Diagonal Symphony,* Richter composed his *Rhythm 21* of squares in black, grey and white. One year later, Walter Ruttmann, also a painter, joined in the trend with *Opus 1,* which was a dynamic display of spots vaguely recalling X-ray photographs. As the titles reveal, the authors themselves considered their products a sort of optical music. It was a

talline compositions.[11] In addition, the ornamental system in *Caligari* expanded through space, annulling its conventional aspect by means of painted shadows in disharmony with the lighting effects, and zigzag delineations designed to efface all rules of perspective. Space now dwindled to a flat plane, now augmented its dimensions to become what one writer called a ' stereoscopic universe.'[12]

Lettering was introduced as an essential element of the settings — appropriately enough, considering the close relationship between lettering and drawing. In one scene the mad psychiatrist's desire to imitate Caligari materialises in jittery characters composing the words ' I must become Caligari ' — words that loom before his eyes on the road, in the clouds, in the treetops. The incorporation of human beings and their movements into the texture of these surroundings was tremendously difficult. Of all the players only

music that, whatever else it tried to impart, marked an utter withdrawal from the outer world. This esoteric avant-garde movement soon spread over other countries. From about 1924, such advanced French artists as Fernard Léger and René Clair made films which, less abstract than the German ones, showed an affinity for the formal beauty of machine parts, and moulded all kinds of objects and motions into surrealistic dreams. — I feel indebted to Mr. Hans Richter for having permitted me to use his unpublished manuscript, ' Avant-garde, History and Dates of the Only Independent Artistic Film Movement, 1921–1931.' See also *Film Society Programme,* October 16, 1927; Kurtz, *Expressionismus* pp 86, 94; Vincent, *Histoire de l'Art Cinématographique,* pp 159–61; Man Ray, ' Answer to a Questionnaire,' *Film Art,* No. 7, 1936, p 9; Kraszna-Krausz, ' Exhibition in Stuttgart, June 1929, and Its Effects,' *Close Up,* December 1929, pp 461–62.

[11] Mr. Feininger wrote to me about his relation to *Caligari* on September 13, 1944: ' Thank you for your . . . letter of September 8. But if there has been anything I never had a part in nor the slightest knowledge of at the time, it is the film *Caligari.* I have never even seen the film . . . I never met nor knew the artists you name [Warm, Röhrig and Reimann] who devised the settings. Some time about 1911 I made, for my own edification, a series of drawings which I entitled: ' Die Stadt am Ende der Welt.' Some of these drawings were printed, some were exhibited. Later, after the birth of *Caligari,* I was frequently asked whether I had had a hand in its devising. This is all I can tell you. . . .'

[12] Cited by Carter, *The New Spirit,* p 250, from H. G. Scheffauer, *The New Spirit in the German Arts.* — For the *Caligari* décor, see also Kurtz, *Expressionismus,* p 66; Rotha, *Film Till Now,* p 46; Jahier, ' 42 Ans de Cinéma,' *Le Rôle Intellectuel du Cinéma,* pp 60–61; ' The Cabinet of Dr. Caligari,' *Exceptional Photoplays,* March 1921, p 4; Amiguet, *Cinéma! Cinéma!* p 50. For the beginnings of Werner Krauss and Conrad Veidt, see Kalbus, *Deutsche Filmkunst,* 1, 28, 30, and Veidt, ' Mein Leben,' *Ufa-Magazin,* January 14–20, 1927.

the two protagonists seemed actually to be created by a draftsman's imagination. Werner Krauss as Caligari had the appearance of a phantom magician himself weaving the lines and shades through which he paced, and when Conrad Veidt's Cesare prowled along a wall, it was as if the wall had exuded him. The figure of an old dwarf and the crowd's antiquated costumes helped to remove the throng on the fair's tent-street from reality and make it share the bizarre life of abstract forms.

If Decla had chosen to leave the original story of Mayer and Janowitz as it was, these 'drawings brought to life' would have told it perfectly. As expressionist abstractions they were animated by the same revolutionary spirit that impelled the two script-writers to accuse authority — the kind of authority revered in Germany — of inhuman excesses. However, Wiene's version disavowed this revolutionary meaning of expressionist staging, or, at least, put it, like the original story itself, in brackets. In the film *Caligari* expressionism seems to be nothing more than the adequate translation of a madman's fantasy into pictorial terms. This was how many contemporary German reviewers understood, and relished, the settings and gestures. One of the critics stated with self-assured ignorance, 'The idea of rendering the notions of sick brains . . . through expressionist pictures is not only well conceived but also well realised. Here this style has a right to exist, proves an outcome of solid logic.'[13]

In their triumph the philistines overlooked one significant fact: even though *Caligari* stigmatised the oblique chimneys as crazy, it never restored the perpendicular ones as the normal. Expressionist ornaments also overrun the film's concluding episode, in which, from the philistines' viewpoint, perpendiculars should have been expected to characterise the revival of conventional reality. In consequence, the *Caligari* style was as far from depicting madness as it was from transmitting revolutionary messages. What function did it really assume?

During the postwar years expressionism was frequently considered a shaping of primitive sensations and experiences. Gerhart Hauptmann's brother Carl — a distinguished writer and poet with

---

[13] Review in *8 Uhr Abendblatt,* cited in *Caligari-Heft,* p 8.

expressionist inclinations — adopted this definition and then asked how the spontaneous manifestations of a profoundly agitated soul might best be formulated. While modern language, he contended, is too perverted to serve this purpose, the film — or the bioscop, as he termed it — offers a unique opportunity to externalise the fermentation of inner life. Of course, he said, the bioscop must feature only those gestures of things and of human beings which are truly soulful.[14]

Carl Hauptmann's views elucidate the expressionist style of *Caligari*. It had the function of characterising the phenomena on the screen as phenomena of the soul — a function which overshadowed its revolutionary meaning. By making the film an outward projection of psychological events, expressionist staging symbolised — much more strikingly than did the device of a framing story — that general retreat into a shell which occurred in postwar Germany. It is not accidental that, as long as this collective process was effective, odd gestures and settings in an expressionist or similar style marked many a conspicuous film. *Variety,* of 1925, showed the final traces of them. Owing to their stereotyped character, these settings and gestures were like some familiar street sign — ' Men at Work,' for instance. Only here the lettering was different. The sign read ' Soul at Work.'

After a thorough propaganda campaign culminating in the puzzling poster, ' You must become Caligari,' Decla released the film in February 1920 in the Berlin Marmorhaus.[15] Among the press reviews — they were unanimous in praising *Caligari* as the first work of art on the screen — that of *Vorwärts,* the leading Social Democratic Party organ, distinguished itself by utter absurdity. It commented upon the film's final scene, in which the director of the asylum promises to heal Francis, with the words: ' This film is also morally invulnerable inasmuch as it evokes sympathy for the mentally diseased, and comprehension for the self-sacrificing activity of the psychiatrists and attendants.'[16] Instead of

---

[14] Carl Hauptmann, ' Film and Theater,' *Der Film von Morgen,* p 20. See also Alten, ' Die Kunst in Deutschland,' *Ganymed,* 1920, p 146; Kurtz, *Expressionismus,* p 14.

[15] *Jahrbuch der Filmindustrie,* 1922–23, p 31.

[16] Quoted from *Caligari-Heft,* p 23.

recognising that Francis' attack against an odious authority harmonised with the party's own anti-authoritarian doctrine, *Vorwärts* preferred to pass off authority itself as a paragon of progressive virtues. It was always the same psychological mechanism: the rationalised middle-class propensities of the Social Democrats interfering with their rational socialist designs. While the Germans were too close to *Caligari* to appraise its symptomatic value, the French realised that this film was more than just an exceptional film. They coined the term ' *Caligarisme* ' and applied it to a postwar world seemingly all upside down; which, at any rate, proves that they sensed the film's bearing on the structure of society. The New York première of *Caligari,* in April 1921, firmly established its world fame. But apart from giving rise to stray imitations and serving as a yardstick for artistic endeavours, this ' most widely discussed film of the time ' never seriously influenced the course of the American or French cinema.[17] It stood out lonely, like a monolith.

Caligari shows the ' Soul at Work.' On what adventures does the revolutionised soul embark? The narrative and pictorial elements of the film gravitate toward two opposite poles. One can be labelled ' Authority,' or, more explicitly, ' Tyranny.' The theme of tyranny, with which the authors were obsessed, pervades the screen from beginning to end. Swivel chairs of enormous height symbolise the superiority of the city officials turning on them, and, similarly, the gigantic back of the chair in Alan's attic testifies to the invisible presence of powers that have their grip on him. Staircases reinforce the effect of the furniture: numerous steps ascend to police headquarters, and in the lunatic asylum itself no less than three parallel flights of stairs are called upon to mark Dr. Caligari's position at the top of the hierarchy. That the film succeeds in picturing him as a tyrant figure of the stamp of Homunculus and Lubitsch's Henry VIII is substantiated by a most illuminating statement in Joseph Freeman's novel, *Never Call Retreat.* Its hero, a Viennese professor of history, tells of his life in a German concentration camp where, after being tortured, he is thrown into a cell:

' Lying alone in that cell, I thought of Dr. Caligari; then, without transition, of the Emperor Valentinian, master of the Roman

---
[17] Quotation from Jacobs, *American Film,* p 303; see also pp 304–5.

21

world, who took great delight in imposing the death sentence for slight or imaginary offences. This Caesar's favourite expressions were : " Strike off his head ! " — " Burn him alive ! " — " Let him be beaten with clubs till he expires ! " I thought what a genuine twentieth-century ruler the emperor was, and promptly fell asleep.'[18]

This dreamlike reasoning penetrates Dr. Caligari to the core by conceiving him as a counterpart of Valentinian and a premonition of Hitler. Caligari is a very specific premonition in the sense that he uses hypnotic power to force his will upon his tool — a technique foreshadowing, in content and purpose, that manipulation of the soul which Hitler was the first to practice on a gigantic scale. Even though, at the time of *Caligari,* the motif of the masterful hypnotiser was not unknown on the screen — it played a prominent role in the American film *Trilby,* shown in Berlin during the war — nothing in their environment invited the two authors to feature it.[19] They must have been driven by one of those dark impulses which, stemming from the slowly moving foundations of a people's life, sometimes engender true visions.

One should expect the pole opposing that of tyranny to be the pole of freedom; for it was doubtless their love of freedom which made Janowitz and Mayer disclose the nature of tyranny. Now this counterpole is the rallying point of elements pertaining to the fair — the fair with its rows of tents, its confused crowds besieging them, and its diversity of thrilling amusements. Here Francis and Alan join the swarm of onlookers; here, on the scene of his triumphs, Dr. Caligari is finally trapped. In their attempts to define the character of a fair, literary sources repeatedly evoke the memory of Babel and Babylon alike. A seventeenth-century pamphlet describes the noise typical of a fair as ' such a distracted noise that you would think Babel not comparable to it,' and, almost two hundred years later, a young English poet feels enthusiastic about ' that Babylon of booths — the Fair.'[20] The manner in which such Biblical images insert themselves unmistakably characterises the fair as an enclave of anarchy in the sphere of entertainment.

[18] Freeman, *Never Call Retreat,* p 528.
[19] Kalbus, *Deutsche Filmkunst,* 1, 95.
[20] McKechnie, *Popular Entertainments,* pp 33, 47.

This accounts for its eternal attractiveness. People of all classes and ages enjoy losing themselves in a wilderness of glaring colours and shrill sounds, which is populated with monsters and abounding in bodily sensations — from violent shocks to tastes of incredible sweetness. For adults it is a regression into childhood days, in which games and serious affairs are identical, real and imagined things mingle, and anarchical desires aimlessly test infinite possibilities. By means of this regression the adult escapes a civilisation which tends to overgrow and starve out the chaos of instincts — escapes it to restore that chaos upon which civilisation nevertheless rests. The fair is not freedom, but anarchy entailing chaos.

Significantly, most fair scenes in *Caligari* open with a small iris-in exhibiting an organ-grinder whose arm constantly rotates, and, behind him, the top of a merry-go-round which never ceases its circular movement.[21] The circle here becomes a symbol of chaos. While freedom resembles a river, chaos resembles a whirlpool. Forgetful of self, one may plunge into chaos; one cannot move on in it. That the two authors selected a fair with its liberties as contrast to the oppressions of Caligari betrays the flaw in their revolutionary aspirations. Much as they longed for freedom, they were apparently incapable of imagining its contours. There is something Bohemian in their conception; it seems the product of naïve idealism rather than true insight. But it might be said that the fair faithfully reflected the chaotic condition of postwar Germany.

Whether intentionally or not, *Caligari* exposes the soul wavering between tyranny and chaos, and facing a desperate situation : any escape from tyranny seems to throw it into a state of utter confusion. Quite logically, the film spreads an all-pervading atmosphere of horror. Like the Nazi world, that of *Caligari* overflows with sinister portents, acts of terror and outbursts of panic. The equation of horror and hopelessness comes to a climax in the final episode, which pretends to re-establish normal life.

Except for the ambiguous figure of the director and the shadowy

---

[21] Rotha, *Film Till Now*, p 285. For the role of fairs in films, see E. W. and M. M. Robson, *The Film Answers Back*, pp 196-7. — An iris-in is a technical term for opening up the scene from a small circle of light in a dark screen until the whole frame is revealed.

members of his staff, normality realises itself through the crowd of insane moving in their bizarre surroundings. The normal as a madhouse : frustration could not be pictured more finally. And in this film, as well as in *Homunculus,* is unleashed a strong sadism and an appetite for destruction. The reappearance of these traits on the screen once more testifies to their prominence in the German collective soul.

Technical peculiarities betray peculiarities of meaning. In *Caligari* methods begin to assert themselves which belong among the special properties of German film technique. *Caligari* initiates a long procession of 100 per cent studio-made films. Whereas, for instance, the Swedes at that time went to great pains to capture the actual appearance of a snowstorm or a wood, the German directors, at least until 1924, were so infatuated with indoor effects that they built up whole landscapes within the studio walls. They preferred the command of an artificial universe to dependence upon a haphazard outer world. Their withdrawal into the studio was part of the general retreat into a shell. Once the Germans had determined to seek shelter within the soul, they could not well allow the screen to explore that very reality which they abandoned. This explains the conspicuous role of architecture after *Caligari* — a role that has struck many an observer. ' It is of the utmost importance,' Paul Rotha remarks in a survey of the postwar period, ' to grasp the significant part played by the architect in the development of the German cinema.'[22] How could it be otherwise? The architect's façades and rooms were not merely backgrounds, but hieroglyphs. They expressed the structure of the soul in terms of space.

Caligari also mobilises light. It is a lighting device which enables the spectators to watch the murder of Alan without seeing it; what they see, on the wall of the student's attic, is the shadow of Cesare stabbing that of Alan. Such devices developed into a speciality of the German studios. Jean Cassou credits the Germans with having invented a ' laboratory-made fairy illumination,'[23] and Harry Alan

[22] Rotha, *Film Till Now,* p 180. Cf Potamkin, ' Kino and Lichtspiel,' *Close Up,* November 1929, p 387.
[23] Cited in Leprohon, ' Le Cinéma Allemand,' *Le Rouge et le Noir,* July 1928, p 135.

Potamkin considers the handling of the light in the German film its 'major contribution to the cinema.'[24] This emphasis upon light can be traced to an experiment Max Reinhardt made on the stage shortly before *Caligari*. In his *mise-en-scène* of Sorge's prewar drama *The Beggar* (*Der Bettler*) — one of the earliest and most vigorous manifestations of expressionism — he substituted for normal settings imaginary ones created by means of lighting effects.[25] Reinhardt doubtless introduced these effects to be true to the drama's style. The analogy to the films of the postwar period is obvious : it was their expressionist nature which impelled many a German director of photography to breed shadows as rampant as weeds and associate ethereal phantoms with strangely lit arabesques or faces. These efforts were designed to bathe all scenery in an unearthly illumination marking it as scenery of the soul. 'Light has breathed soul into the expressionist films,' Rudolph Kurtz states in his book on the expressionist cinema.[26] Exactly the reverse holds true : in those films the soul was the virtual source of the light. The task of switching on this inner illumination was somewhat facilitated by powerful romantic traditions.

The attempt made in *Caligari* to co-ordinate settings, players, lighting and action is symptomatic of the sense of structural organisation which, from this film on, manifests itself on the German screen. Rotha coins the term 'studio constructivism' to characterise 'that curious air of completeness, of finality, that surrounds each product of the German studios.'[27] But organisational completeness can be achieved only if the material to be organised does not object to it. (The ability of the Germans to organise themselves owes much to their longing for submission.) Since reality is essentially incalculable and therefore demands to be observed rather than commanded, realism on the screen and total organisation exclude each other. Through their 'studio constructivism' no less

---

[24] Potamkin, 'The Rise and Fall of the German Film, *Cinema,* April 1930, p 24.
[25] Kurtz, *Expressionismus,* p 59.
[26] Ibid, p 60.
[27] Rotha, *Film Till Now,* pp 107–8. Cf Potamkin, 'Kino and Lichtspiel,' *Close Up,* November 1929, p 388, and 'The Rise and Fall of the German Film,' *Cinema,* April 1930, p 24.

than their lighting the German films revealed that they dealt with unreal events displayed in a sphere basically controllable.[28]

In the course of a visit to Paris about six years after the première of *Caligari,* Janowitz called on Count Etienne de Beaumont in his old city residence, where he lived among Louis Seize furniture and Picassos. The Count voiced his admiration of *Caligari,* terming it ' as fascinating and abstruse as the German soul.' He continued, ' Now the time has come for the German soul to speak, monsieur. The French soul spoke more than a century ago, in the Revolution, and you have been mute. . . . Now we are waiting for what you have to impart to us, to the world.'[29]

The Count did not have long to wait.

---

[28] Film connoisseurs have repeatedly criticised *Caligari* for being a stage imitation. This aspect of the film partly results from its genuinely theatrical action. It is action of a well-constructed dramatic conflict in stationary surroundings — action which does not depend upon screen representation for significance. Like *Caligari,* all ' indoor ' films of the postwar period showed affinity for the stage in that they favoured inner-life dramas at the expense of conflicts involving outer reality. However, this did not necessarily prevent them from growing into true films. When, in the wake of *Caligari,* film technique steadily progressed, the psychological screen dramas increasingly exhibited an imagery that elaborated the significance of their action. *Caligari's* theatrical affinity was also due to technical backwardness. An immovable camera focused upon the painted décor; no cutting device added a meaning of its own to that of the pictures. One should, of course, not forget the reciprocal influence *Caligari* and kindred films exerted, for their part, on the German stage. Stimulated by the use they made of the iris-in, stage lighting took to singling out a lone player, or some important sector of the scene. Cf Barry, *Program Notes,* Series III, Program 1 ; Gregor *Zeitalter des Films,* pp 134, 144–45 ; Rotha, *Film Till Now,* p 275 ; Vincent, *Histoire de l'Art Cinématographique,* p 139.
[29] From Janowitz's manuscript.

CARL MAYER'S DEBUT

by Erich Pommer

It was about a year after the end of the first World War. Within this year I had organised a small film studio, Decla, in Berlin and I was quite pleased with the way things were going — in spite of all the post-war restrictions on money and materials and electric power. Our most valuable assets were our enthusiasm and our ingenuity.

The enterprise didn't leave anyone much time for relaxation, so I used the lunch hour as my rest period. During this lunch hour, one day, there was a timid knock on my office door — which I didn't bother to answer. Nevertheless, the door was pushed open, and when the two young fellows there saw that someone was in the room, they knocked again, and asked for Mr. Pommer.

I said, ' I don't think you can see him to-day.'

They took turns speaking. ' We have a story that we're sure would interest him.'

' Mr. Pommer is a very busy man — leave your story — I'll see that it gets to him.'

' No, sir, we can't do that. We know that when we submit it officially, it just goes through a lot of secretaries (pardon!) — so we're determined to read it to him personally.'

' I'm *sorry*.'

But they weren't giving up yet. ' That's a shame. We have a lot of ideas, but we never seem able to reach the right man — and this idea is really something new — *different*.'

I tried another tack, to get rid of them. ' I'll let you into a secret. I'm Pommer, but I can't listen to any stories to-day. Can't you leave it with me?'

'Please give us just ten minutes — if you don't like what we've told you at the end of ten minutes, stop us, and we'll leave.'

They stayed three hours, and before they left I had written them a cheque for 800 marks. They called their story *The Cabinet of Dr. Caligari*. The two boys (I felt they were boys, even though I was only about five years older) were both from Prague. Carl Mayer was working as a *Dramaturg* (a combination play-reader and textual editor) at a small theatre on the Blumenstrasse. It was his collaborator, Hans Janowitz, who had had the idea for the story, after seeing a newspaper item about a Hamburg murderer. Janowitz and Mayer had developed the incident into a story that they insisted must be executed in a definite style.

The artist whose style they wanted followed was Alfred Kubin, the hero of Prague's radical artists. While Mayer and Janowitz talked about art, I was thinking of rather different aspects of the script. The mystery and macabre atmosphere of the Grand Guignol was currently in vogue in German films, and this story fitted perfectly. They saw an 'experiment' in the script — I saw a comparatively inexpensive production.

There was a pause for four or five months before the actual filming was planned. Wiene was considering directing it. The boys tried to get Kubin excited in their project. In the meantime I put them into work on another fantastic mystery idea, and put *Caligari* in the hands of the three artists who constituted Decla's designing staff — Warm, Herlth, and Röhrig, whom I had met as a soldier painting sets for a German military theatre in Braila, Rumania.

The studio had a very limited quota of power and light, and on the day when we were notified that we had exhausted the month's quota (several days before the end of the month), my three artists brought in a proposition that seemed to me absurd, and even reactionary — 'Why not paint lights and shadows on the sets for this *Caligari* film?'

When I protested against this return to primitive film-making, Herlth (the quietest of the three) made his statement, 'Look here, Mr. Pommer, we are living in an age of expressionism, and in painting these sets in this style, we can do a great deal more in emphasising the important elements of the story.'

'Look here, boys, you're all crazy. It's impossible to put fantastic, unreal, flat sets behind real, solid people.'

The next day they brought me a series of drawings, which they probably had had all along, but hadn't wanted to frighten me with the day before. When I remained unconvinced, they coaxed me into letting Wiene make a test scene. When the test was screened, both Mayer and Janowitz were present. We were all convinced — and the writers dropped their efforts to engage Kubin. In fact, they were so impressed that they wrote their second script with this new method in mind, which may be the reason *Genuine* was so bad a film.

The Cabinet of Dr. Caligari cannot be called a typical Carl Mayer script, but it did serve to introduce him to his true medium. During its production the young writers saw each day's rushes, a habit that Mayer maintained throughout his screen-writing career. His powerful visual imagination was kept constantly stimulated by close contact with the entire production process — and from *Caligari* can be dated Mayer's well-known awareness of the camera and settings as vital dramatic elements.

Other writers wrote (and still write) scripts that have to be translated into film terms. Carl Mayer wrote true film-scripts and, in so doing, inspired all film artists who worked in that famous post-war period of German cinema.

CARL MAYER — AN APPRECIATION

by Paul Rotha

Most writers who work in films are already writers of books and plays, or, at the least, they are journalists. Carl Mayer never wrote a play, a book or an article. He wrote only in film terms. He was an integral product of the medium he loved and understood so well.

Through Robert Flaherty, I first met Carl Mayer, in London, in 1936, but I had respected the name since the early '20s. It had been a script credit on some of the famous German films of what has been called the Golden Period. In Berlin in 1931, I had heard his name spoken with reverence; but it was only later, when I came to know him so well and after I talked with many famous contributors to early German cinema, that I realised the full extent of his influence.

He was born at Graz, Austria, in 1894, one of three brothers. He wanted to be an actor, then a painter, but became a kind of story-editor at a theatre. In Berlin in 1919 he conceived *The Cabinet of Dr. Caligari*. Of that conception I wrote in detail in *World Film News*, September, 1938.

Caligari and *Genuine* were the only two films to use expressionist painted backgrounds. This was not Mayer's idea, but that of the designers, Warm, Reimann, Röhrig. If you look at *Caligari* to-day, you respect it not so much for its sets or its formalised acting but for its conception, and the way the camera is used to present the madman's outlook on the world. For Carl Mayer saw everything through the camera. It was the flow of images, the creation of atmosphere by selected details, the expression of character by visual means, that compelled him to write films which refused to use printed subtitles to tell their story. With most other films, claim for this masterly technique would be given to the director, but because of his method of script-writing, Carl Mayer must take the major credit. His scripts were written in infinite detail, with meticulous instructions to director and cameraman. He frequently presided at the shooting and always had final say in the editing. His script of *Sunrise* is circulated to this day in Hollywood as a model of structure and continuity.

In the same way that he found himself logically writing scripts without sub-titles, so he came to suggest the moving camera. That was in *New Year's Eve*. The camera had, it is true, been put on motor cars and trains before that, but usually only for novelty's sake. Reminiscing, Carl told me many times how he fought with the problems of expressing time in that film. The clock in the town square dominated the story, which told the events minute by minute in the hour preceding midnight. 'Through the pages of my manuscript,' he said, ' the face of the clock tower moved closer and closer towards me. It had to *move, to grow bigger*. So the camera had to move. Guido Seeber mounted it on a perambulator. It was so obvious.' The next year, he gave full vent to this new idea, and with the help of Karl Freund, *The Last Laugh* was a revolution in moving camera work. Its showing in America led to the ubiquitous use of the camera-dolly and the crane, now built with such elaborate mechanism and so often used without real cinematic reason.

From a story aspect, Mayer's great contribution was his choice of subject and characters. One must remember that the really popular German films in 1920–24 were the lavish spectacular pictures, imitations of the Italian *Salammbo,* and *Cabiria*. Successes of the day were *Anne Boleyn, Dubarry, Sumurun,* and *The Lovers of Pharaoh*, some of them financed by Hugenberg as anti-allied propaganda. Set against this *kitsch,* Carl Mayer's simple, warm, human approach to the relationship of a few individuals — usually drawn from a lower middle-class environment, often concentrated on the story of a single character — was a new sociological use of cinema. *Berlin* was also his conception, but he disliked Ruttmann's inhuman handling of the idea and asked for his name to be removed from the credits. Few of these films were commercially successful if compared with the flamboyant romances, but they were the films that made Germany famous. It was to their creators that Hollywood offered big contracts: Murnau, Gliese, Lubitsch, Freund, Leni, Veidt, Jannings; most of them sacrificed themselves on

31

the Hollywood machine. To Carl Mayer, whose script of *The Last Laugh* was studied so enviously in America, Fox made a handsome offer to write *Sunrise*. He wrote it, in his own good time; but he wrote it in Europe and stubbornly resisted going to Hollywood.

He was a careful, patient worker. He would take days over a few shots, a year or more over a script. He would wrestle and fight with his problems all day and all night. He would go long, lonely walks with them. He would never deliver a script until he was wholly satisfied that the problems were solved. He would rather cancel his contract and return the money than be forced to finish a script in the wrong way. He had iron principles arising from the film medium itself, and never once departed from them. His instinct and love for film dominated his way of living. Film mattered most and he gave everything, including his health, to it.

To Paris he went with Elisabeth Bergner and Czinner in the early sound-film days, and with them he worked on several films — *Der Träumende Mund* and *Ariane*. He came to England in 1932 and began a twelve-year period of helping others. He took no screen credits here, except only on the documentary films made of *The Times* newspaper in '38 and '39, but did advisory work on *Pygmalion* and *Major Barbara* among others. His script of the East End nobody would produce. His fascinating idea of translating Goldsmith's *She Stoops to Conquer* remained only an idea in script form. He gave much time to criticising scripts and cutting copies at my unit, and no technician can have failed to learn from him if they so wanted. To *World of Plenty* he contributed a great deal. Of the big commercial companies, only Two Cities recognised his talent and for them that last year, thanks to del Guidice, he acted as consultant. A few weeks before his death he received a letter from Dr. Siegfried Kracauer, from New York, who was writing for the Guggenheim Foundation a book on the social and political background of the great German films.[1] Kracauer had realised the great influence of Carl Mayer; almost every German film of the Golden Period leads back to his inspiration.

Such men in this mad, money-crazy industry of ours are rare.

---

[1] *From Caligari to Hitler,* Siegfried Kracauer (Princetown University Press, 1947).

Had he craved a fortune, his name in tall letters, Carl could have had it at a price he was not prepared to pay — liberty to write as and how he believed. He loved life with a happiness you do not normally find among film-makers. He loved all films and could find something to talk about in the worst of pictures. Above all, he loved people — the people he met in cafés and trains and parks. He seldom read books, and possessed but a dozen connected with subjects on which he was working. He devoured newspapers. His little money he gave away to make others happy.

They are nearly all dead — that group which made German films so famous. Of them all, Carl Mayer's name will remain longest, for from him they drew their inspiration. He belonged to films like no man before him; his body died, July 1st, 1944, from cancer; his name and work will live on.

CREDITS:

Original story and screenplay by	Carl Mayer and Hans Janowitz
Directed by	Robert Wiene
Produced by	Erich Pommer
Production Company	Decla Film, Berlin
Settings designed by	Hermann Warm, Walter Reimann and Walter Röhrig
Photography by	Willy Hameister
Process	Black and white (Originally tinted in green, brown and steely-blue)
Length	4,682 feet
First shown in Berlin	February 1920

CAST:

Dr. Caligari	Werner Krauss
Cesare	Conrad Veidt
Francis	Friedrich Feher
Jane	Lil Dagover
Alan	Hans Heinz von Twardowski
Dr. Olson	Rudolf Lettinger
A criminal	Rudolph Klein-Rogge

THE CABINET
OF
DR. CALIGARI

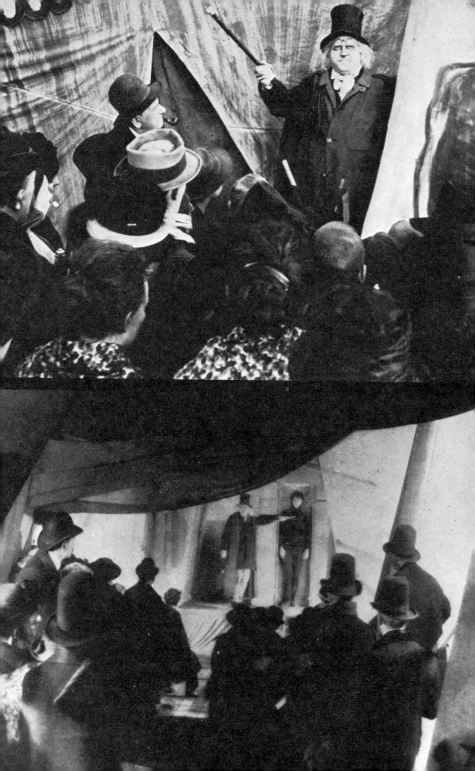

THE CABINET OF DR. CALIGARI

A cold, sombre atmosphere pervades the opening scene of the film. Francis and an older man are sitting on a bench by a high forbidding wall which curves away into shadow. The leafless branches and twigs of a tree hang down above the heads of the two men; dead leaves carpet a path in front of them, emphasising the lifeless, still quality of the setting. On the opposite side of the path to the bench are a couple of stunted fir-trees: winter is in the air. Both of the men on the bench are dressed in black; their eyes gape wildly from pale faces. The older man leans over towards his young companion to speak to him; Francis, apparently not very interested, responds by staring blankly skyward. (Still on page 17)

As he turns to speak to Francis, the eyes of the older man, beneath a pair of bushy grey eyebrows, are dilated with horror or fear.

TITLE: '*Everywhere there are spirits . . . They are all around us . . . They have driven me from hearth and home, from my wife and children.*'

The older man continues his monologue, while the boughs from the overhanging tree move about his face. We see that the wall behind him is painted with a bizarre leaf and line pattern.

Francis turns suddenly to look down the path past his older friend. As he turns he makes a sudden movement of surprise: the figure of a young woman, Jane, has just emerged from the shadow at the end of the path. She walks down the path towards camera; her hair is long and black, framing a pale, utterly expressionless face; her long white *décolleté* gown trails about her as she walks slowly forward. (Still on page 17)

Francis stares at the passing girl with a mixture of anxiety and admiration.

Jane draws closer to the two men; she is still staring blankly in front of her. As she draws levels with them Francis leans forward even further across his companion, rises slightly from his seat and points

41

towards the girl.

Francis's face registers adulation and tenderness as the girl passes him by; he is very excited and moved by her presence.

The girl walks straight past the men, giving no sign that she has seen them. They continue to stare at her intently, a certain element of amazement in their looks, but she passes without a flicker of recognition, parting the trailing branches of an overhanging tree and finally disappears. The men stare after her, a dazed look on their faces.

Francis, still gazing after Jane inclines his head meaningfully towards his companion, as though about to make a momentous announcement.

TITLE : ' *That is my fiancée.*'

Francis's face becomes very animated as he talks rapidly to his friend, still gazing pathetically after the departed woman.

The two men stare, fascinated, after the departed girl. (Still on page 18)

The girl gazes vacantly upward and right, her white gown standing out strongly against an indistinct dark background. She turns slowly to face camera and begins to move forward towards it. As she comes closer it is possible to see that her face is dead white, with heavily made-up eyes.

Both the men now have expressions of surprise on their faces. Francis is pointing in the direction in which Jane has vanished.

The heads of the two men have moved closer together as their conversation becomes more intimate; Francis turns towards the older man.

TITLE : ' *What she and I have experienced is yet more remarkable than the story you have told me. I will tell you . . .*'

The two men put their heads closer together; Francis continues talking.

Jane, her white gown flowing about her, is walking behind a screen of fir-tree branches, which are silhouetted against the whiteness of the garment. Slowly and pensively, she continues her walk.

Francis stretches out his hand in front of him as if about to display something to the older man.

TITLE : *'Holstenwall, the small town where I was born.'*

The two men, their heads close together, look right.
A painted townscape : the town is built all over a sharply pointed hill; we have the impression of closely packed houses with pointed rooftops and gables clinging precariously to the sides of the steeply rising hill. On the peak of the hill is a large church with two steeples which lean crazily inwards towards one another.

TITLE : *'A travelling fair had arrived.'*

Painted scene of tents and roundabouts in the foreground; in the background are the houses of the town on the hill. The tents are suggested by a confusion of angled planes and surfaces on which scallop shapes have been picked out in a lighter colour to represent festoons and hangings. In front of the tents is a flat white platform, behind which there is a line of railings with a sloping banister rail, suggesting the top of a flight of steps.
Francis and his companion are still deep in conversation on the bench by the wall. Francis continues talking, raising his hand in the grip of strong emotion. An expression of horror and loathing begins to creep into his already dilated eyes.

TITLE : *'With it, came a scoundrel . . .'*

The top-hatted figure of Dr. Caligari appears walking up the flight of steps in the centre of the fairground setting; he is clutching at the banister-rail. When he reaches the top of the steps, he turns towards camera. His black cloak is tightly wrapped around him; he peers quizzically, irascibly, around him through large round spectacles, then hobbles painfully forward, leaning heavily on his stick with one hand and carrying a book in the other. He is wearing white gloves, on the back of which are painted three broad black stripes, extensions of the spaces between his fingers. Hobbling forward, he looks a sinister, menacing cripple, capable of the utmost evil. His lips are tightly pursed and he glares wildly ahead; his white hair straggles out from beneath the brim of his hat. Iris out on Caligari's face, leaning back slightly as if sniffing the atmosphere. We return to the two men sitting by the wall. Francis, hollow-eyed, is staring dramatically heavenward :

TITLE : ' *Alan, my friend.*'

Alan, a young man of aesthetic pursuits, lives in an attic, which is suggested by sloping walls and a kite-shaped dormer window, giving on to angular rooftops and crazily-leaning chimneys. Alan's bed is half hidden in shadow on right. In front of the bed in the centre of the room is a high ladder-back chair. Alan stands affectedly by his desk reading a book. Just behind him is a star-shaped patch of light painted on the floor. He walks forward, still deeply engrossed in his reading, and absent-mindedly stretches out his arm to lean on the back of the chair.

Alan's face suggests a deeply-serious, well-intentioned young man — a man of high ideals, though a jutting chin perhaps indicates a certain determination in achieving them. He affects the style of the Nineties aesthete — a loosely-tied, flopping bow-tie and hair parted in the centre in the style of Aubrey Beardsley. One arm rests on the back of the chair and he holds his book open with the other. He suddenly looks up impatiently and turns towards the window.

Alan turns away from the chair, thoughtfully closing his book, and walks towards the window in the rear wall of his room.

He gazes out through the window over the crazily angled rooftops and chimneys, then turns away, face tilted slightly upwards and eyes lit up with a radiant smile.

He moves forward, away from the window, rubbing his hands together gleefully, and suddenly leaves the room. Camera remains on the room for a few moments, before Alan re-enters with his coat slung casually over one shoulder and his hat in his hand. He crosses the room and leaves.

In the street a man is energetically distributing handbills to passers-by. Alan, now wearing his hat and coat, enters from left and walks towards the man who gives him one of the handbills. Behind the two men is a painted facade of a house leaning at a crazy angle; in the left foreground a flight of steps disappears upwards into shadow. Handbill in hand and reading avidly, Alan turns towards camera.

> *LATE EXTRA!*
> *Holstenwall Fair,*
> *including sideshows of all*
> *kinds, and marvels never*
> *before seen.*

Alan, still reading his handbill walks slowly forward, then suddenly turns and darts up the steps.

Alan dashes into Francis's room brandishing the handbill. Francis is sitting at his desk working quietly; a book-case stands just behind the desk against the wall. There is a triangular-shaped window in the rear wall of the room; in the foreground is a large leather sofa. As Alan runs in from the left, Francis turns to see what all the commotion is about. Alan perches on the arm of Francis's chair and starts talking energetically and gesturing towards the door with the handbill, as though urging Francis to come with him to the fair. Francis takes the handbill and the two friends rise to their feet to read it together.

Alan is pulling urgently at Francis's arm; Francis smiles as he reads the handbill, as though he feels he has to humour the caprices of his friend. They stand outlined against the strangely shaped window, which we can now see is surrounded by a pattern of pointed streaks.

TITLE : ' *Come on, Francis, let's go to the Fair.*'

Both men are grinning now, and Alan tugs even more vehemently at Francis's arm.

A painted street scene; camera points directly down a very narrow street. The walls of the houses lining the street are suggested by flats painted with stripes and angles. Two men dressed in dark clothes come down the street towards camera and then disappear to left. A woman crosses the street behind them, coming from an opening on the right between two houses and going out to rear. Caligari, his cape wrapped tightly round him, enters at rear and comes down the street at a strange jerky shuffle. (Still on page 18) As he comes towards camera he peers constantly to the right, as though looking for a particular building. Another man appears from left; when

Caligari comes face to face with him, he doffs his hat to the man with an exaggerated gesture of respect and deference, an obsequious look on his face. They talk together animately for a few seconds, then, with a sweep of his right hand, Caligari produces a card which he shows to the man.

TITLE : ' *I shouldn't go in if I were you. The Town Clerk is in a very bad temper today.*'

Caligari, undeterred by this rather cold reception, continues to talk to the man and produces a second card which he gives the man with a mincing gesture, looking very satisfied with himself. The man, visibly impressed, now accepts both cards.
Close-up of a white card with ' DR. CALIGARI ' written boldly on it.
Having accepted the cards the man goes out to left; Caligari shuffles after him, still looking very pleased with himself.
The walls of the Town Clerk's office are painted with fantastic spiked shapes. The Town Clerk is sitting on a very high stool on right; an autocratic-looking man, he is demanding explanations of items in a ledger from two clerks who stand uneasily in front of his stool. At the rear of the office a clerk sits working at a desk. The man with whom Caligari has been talking outside enters on left and hands Caligari's card to the Town Clerk, then leaves again. Caligari himself has followed the man into the office and after the presentation of his card, he doffs his hat and bows low to the Town Clerk, rather overdoing an attempt at humility. The Town Clerk, after looking closely at the card, turns to Caligari angrily.

TITLE : ' *Wait.*'

Visibly put out by the Town Clerk's summary treatment of him, Caligari turns and sits down on the left. The Town Clerk gesticulates angrily at his two subordinates.
Caligari stares malevolently over the top of his spectacles towards the Town Clerk and grasps the top of his cane tightly. His mouth is tightly drawn and his chin juts forward aggressively.
The two clerks exit on left. Caligari, unable to contain his impatience, rises and makes his way towards the Town Clerk with a

46

curious sidelong shuffling movement. He stops just below the Clerk on his high stool; the latter turns angrily to Caligari. (Still on page 19)

TITLE : ' *I told you to wait.* '

Caligari, much chastened by this response, sidles back to the bench on left. The Clerk turns back to the documents on his desk.

Caligari, very disgruntled, turns his face away and looks in the opposite direction to the Clerk.

The Town Clerk gathers up the papers on his desk, which is painted with strange cabbalistic symbols, and descends from his high stool. He straightens his black frock-coat as he climbs down and comes towards camera. Caligari watchfully follows his movements.

Caligari glares intently at the Clerk, his eyes dilated with hatred. He begins to speak, grasping his cane convulsively.

He rises to face the Clerk. The two men make a ludicrous pair together : the very tall Town Clerk towering over the much shorter Caligari, who stands self-effacingly before him, hat and cane in hand.

TITLE : ' *I want to apply for a permit to show my exhibit at the fair.* '

Caligari draws his cane along the floor, as though delineating the size of something. The Town Clerk listens very unwillingly. Throughout this scene Caligari's face is the very picture of craft and cunning.

TITLE : ' *What sort of an exhibit is it?* '

Caligari looks up assertively at the Town Clerk, holding his hat and cane close to his face.

TITLE : ' *A somnambulist.* '

The Town Clerk looks amused. He turns and beckons to the junior clerk who has been sitting at a desk at the rear of the office, before marching pompously out, very conscious of his power to order and influence. The junior clerk comes forward and asks Caligari to follow him to his desk at the rear of the room, which Caligari does, following the clerk in his strange shuffle — half walk, half run.

An arm turning the crank of an organ appears in iris in upper right of screen; on top of the organ a monkey is sitting, wearing a white blouse. The iris opens to reveal the fairground set, with the town on the hill in the background. The fair is now clearly in full swing and people are milling about on the light-coloured platform in the foreground. On the left is a cone-shaped roundabout painted with broad stripes, which is revolving very rapidly. There is another roundabout painted with broad stripes, which is also revolving rapidly. There is another roundabout on the right behind the organ-grinder and the organ. Three men in long dark capes and conical hats come from the left, stop in front of the organ and place money in the little cup held by the monkey. They are followed by a jovial-looking couple who also make a contribution to the monkey's cup; then come a young man and a very prosperous-looking middle-aged man. Caligari enters right, leaning heavily on his cane and hobbling slightly. He turns his back to camera to look at the organ. More people cross the open space in the foreground and place money in the monkey's cup, including a stunted figure, with dwarf's legs but a normal torso. As the figure stops at the organ Caligari turns to look at him, fascinated by the sight, before going towards the rails at the top of the steps in centre of set and turning and glaring balefully around him. (Still on page 20) Finally, he turns away and disappears from sight down the steps.

We are now in another part of the fairground. On either side of a central alleyway are tents with scallop shapes painted on them to represent festoons. A number of people are milling about in the space between the tents, among whom we can recognise the jovial-looking couple who gave money to the organ-grinder. To the right of the central passage is a large marquee with a triangular opening in its side. In front of it is a low platform with railings at each end. A group of small children run in from the right waving pennants. The dwarf comes in from the left carrying a poster, painted with faces and figures in grotesque positions, shaped like a kite and mounted on a standard. He disappears from sight among the people in the alleyway.

Caligari emerges from the triangular opening to the large marquee on the right and steps out on to the low platform. His round spectacles are pushed up on his forehead and he carries a triangular wooden frame mounted on the end of a pole; there is a roll of cloth strapped to the frame. He looks around at the people in the open space in front of the platform of his marquee. He is carrying a large bell in his right hand which he begins to ring, swinging it up and down vigorously.

Attracted by the sound of the bell and the extraordinary sight of Caligari brandishing it wildly, people begin to press round the platform. Caligari unrolls the cloth which he has brought out of the tent to reveal a large painting of an emaciated human figure with a disproportionately large head; it has the manic, tragic face of a painting by Munch.

TITLE : ' *Roll up. Roll up. Now showing for the first time: Cesare, the somnambulist.*'

Caligari harangues the rapidly growing crowd, urging them to come to his show. He strikes the poster furiously with his cane to emphasise his words.

TITLE : ' *That night saw the first of a series of mysterious crimes.*'

Iris in from upper left on the head of two men; iris widens to reveal an attic bedroom. Three men are bending over a bed on the left, looking at the body of a murder victim, though our actual view of the body is blocked by part of the bed. The sheets of the bed and the pillows are in complete disorder and lie partly on the floor, as though a violent struggle had taken place. (Still on page 20) The men draw back from the bed : two uniformed policemen and a plain-clothes inspector. Their faces register horror and consternation.

TITLE : ' *Murder! The Town Clerk has been stabbed in the side by some kind of sharp instrument.*'

The inspector and the two policemen walk away from the bed towards the window at the rear of the room. They gaze out through it, then the inspector turns and speaks to his two subordinates. Iris out. Iris in on the organ-grinder's arm turning the organ crank and the monkey sitting on the organ. Alan and Francis stagger in from right; their arms are round each other's shoulders and they are both smiling broadly, very happy with their visit to the fair. They turn to face camera, look around them, turn and walk away. A group of young women enter from behind the organ and stop in front of it; their arms are linked and they are giggling happily.

Meanwhile, Caligari is still declaiming at the top of his voice from the platform in front of his tent, swinging his bell with both hands. Finally, he puts down the bell, giving him more freedom of movement to gesture towards the poster of the sinister, staring figure. (Still on page 37) In the foreground are the hats of the crowd, many of them conical, as more people press round the platform.

TITLE : ' *Roll up. Roll up. Now showing for the first time: Cesare, the miraculous, twenty-three years of age, has for these three-and-twenty years been sleeping — night and day — without a break. Before your very eyes, Cesare will awaken from his death-like rigidity. Roll up. Roll up.*'

Caligari picks the poster up in one hand and taps it vigorously with his cane to lend weight to his words. Then he puts the poster down and, with a theatrical sweep of his arm, draws back the flap of the tent opening behind him, and invites the people to enter. A number of people climb on to the platform to enter the tent, including the jovial couple we have previously noted. Caligari, not quite satisfied with the response to his showman's cajoling, now removes his hat and makes sweeping gestures with it to urge more people to come to his show. A steady stream of people begin to enter the tent.

The faces of the people in front of the platform are slightly up-turned. In the centre of the group, in angle shot, are Francis and Alan; the latter is speaking eagerly, animatedly, to his friend, urging him to come with him to see the somnambulist. Francis seems dubious and cynical, but Alan still tugs insistently at his arm. Fade in.

TITLE : *The Cabinet of Dr. Caligari.*

Fade out.

Inside Caligari's tent a central aisle leads from foreground to a small stage at rear. The audience for the show are sitting or standing on either side of the aisle. Suddenly a curtain on the right of the stage is swept aside and Caligari bounds on to the stage, ringing his bell and declaiming excitedly. He swiftly gets carried away with the task of his show, casting his bell away to the left. He removes his hat and makes a sweeping bow in front of the curtain, then replaces it and continues his gesticulations with the aid of his cane. Finally he lifts the curtain on the stage and a rope tied round the curtain pulls it away out of sight. Caligari takes up a position in the centre of the stage.

A long narrow cabinet, closely resembling a coffin, is standing on end at the right of the stage. Caligari points towards it vigorously, still shouting to the audience. He reaches up on top of the cabinet and takes down a short stick with which he gestures again towards the doors of the box. Then, with a sudden movement, he flicks open the right door of the cabinet, then the left, to reveal Cesare standing immobile inside. The somnambulist is wearing black tights painted with random oblique stripes and a polo neck sweater. His heavily made-up eyes, which are closed, stand out strongly against a dead-white face. Caligari, spectacles pushed up on forehead, gestures towards Cesare with the short stick. (Still on page 37)

Caligari gazes manically towards the motionless figure of Cesare. He has pulled his spectacles down before his eyes again and his white hair straggles wildly from beneath his top hat.

He turns towards Cesare, whose face, surmounted by an unruly mop of dark hair, looks very pale above his dark clothing.

Caligari glares right towards Cesare. (Still on page 38)

Caligari's excited expression shows that the climax of his show is drawing near.

TITLE : ' *Cesare! Do you hear me? It is I calling you: I, Caligari, your master. Awaken for a brief while from your dark night.*'

Caligari looks up at Cesare expectantly.

Close-up of Cesare's face. He is wearing very heavy white mat make-up, with long eyelashes and thick black lines on his brow. His mouth is painted in the shape of a compressed Cupid's bow. Below each eye is a triangular patch of black make-up. In response to his master's command, the muscles around Cesare's mouth begin to twitch spasmodically, as with someone who is reluctantly coming out of a very deep sleep. His mouth quivers and falls slightly open; his eyelids flutter before parting slowly. Slowly the somnambulist's eyes open wide to a full manic glare, the iris almost entirely surrounded by white.

Caligari makes another gesture towards Cesare, who slowly raises his hands in front of him, fingers extended as though about to strangle someone. Slowly Cesare moves forward, stepping down from the cabinet; as he does so, Caligari shrinks away slightly, feigning apprehension. Cesare lowers his arms and Caligari gestures across the middle with his cane. His spectacles are once more pushed up on his forehead.

Alan and Francis are now in the audience, gazing upwards; their faces are more brightly lit than those of the other people around them. Both of them look somewhat disturbed and anxious about what is taking place on the stage and Alan's mouth has fallen slightly open. He still wears his hat with the floppy brim. He turns and talks agitatedly to Francis.

Caligari, head thrown back and knees slightly bent, is speaking to the audience again. Cesare stands motionless, one foot behind the other in a ballet dancer's pose, hands at his side.

Caligari has begun to grin triumphantly. His spectacles are pushed back on his brow; his eyes gleam and his teeth show as he turns from from one side of the audience to the other. His face lights up with a fiendish grin as he begins to speak again.

TITLE : ' *Ladies and Gentlemen, Cesare will now answer any question you like to put to him. Cesare knows every secret. Cesare knows the past and can see into the future. Come up and test him for yourselves.*'

Caligari bows again and looks admiringly at the wonderful Cesare. Then he turns to the audience again, looking expectantly at them, waiting for their questions.

Alan looks strangely disturbed by Caligari's proposal; he seizes Francis's hands and seems in the grip of some strange impulse, desperately wanting to ask something. Clutching at Alan's right arm, Francis pleads with him not to ask a question. But Alan is absolutely determined to ask Cesare a question and will not be restrained.

Caligari is still posturing on the stage; Cesare's demoniac looks are emphasised by low angle lighting. Alan appears in front of the stage on the left, then crosses to the right of the stage and makes as though to climb on it. Francis comes after him, tugging at his coat and still trying to prevent him from asking his question. Finally, however, Alan manages to climb to the edge of the stage and he addresses himself to Caligari and Cesare.

Alan's face is brightly lit against a dark background — the open face of an honest, naïve young man. His eyebrows are raised questioningly as he prepares to speak.

TITLE : ' How long have I to live? '

Alan's face is upturned and questioning, his brow furrowed.

Francis looks on with apparent horror as Alan asks his question and Cesare makes ready to reply.

Cesare's tousled hair falls over his brow and his eyes are staring wildly. The whiteness of his teeth stands out startlingly in his heavily made-up face. Behind him, a patch of the cabinet is brightly lit. He replies very briefly. (Still on page 38)

TITLE : ' Until tomorrow's dawn.'

Cesare purses his lips after this brief, sinister utterance.

Alan draws back shocked, then smiles, trying to put a good face on things, though clearly very shaken. He draws back, panting as he does so.

Francis stares on, eyes and mouth open in simple-minded disbelief, head tilted right.

A number of the people on either side of the central aisle have risen to their feet. Alan is still standing to the right of the stage. Francis succeeds in dragging him away, however, and the pair come down the aisle towards camera. Alan looks utterly bewildered and he has to be firmly guided by Francis. They go out right.

A street scene; there is a white area on the ground in the centre and the background is composed of house facades leaning at crazy angles. A lamp-lighter emerges from rear right carrying a lamp-lighting pole. His cloak is wrapped tightly round him and he wears a trilby-style hat pushed well back on his head. He crosses the street with a strange lunging gait to light a street lamp before disappearing from sight. (Still on page 39) Two men pass from left to right in front of the houses in the background. Alan and Francis enter and walk to the centre of the space between the houses. Alan's attention is suddenly drawn by a poster on a wall on the left; he grasps his friend's arm and starts towards it.

INSERT: *Holstenwall Murder. 1,000 marks reward.*

Iris in on the poster; iris widens to reveal Alan and Francis gazing intently at it. Alan still looks very upset and Francis has to lead him away from the poster. The two men turn away; as they do so, Francis sees Jane enter in the background and he hurries to greet her. Alan, after a last look at the poster, goes back to join them, circling behind them and halting at Jane's side. (Still on page 39) Alan takes Jane's hand and she in turn takes Francis's hand. They smile, seemingly very happy together. Jane's brows and eyes are heavily made up.

The three friends move forwards towards camera, talking animatedly to each other.

Another street scene in long shot; there is a brightly lit patch in the centre and dark angular forms on either side. A dark alleyway leads off into shadow in the background. A flight of stairs leads upwards at a peculiar angle on the left. Alan, Francis and Jane enter from behind the dark form and walk slowly across the street to the bright patch, pausing an instant and turning to face camera before disappearing behind the form on left. Fast iris down to shadow of a distorted figure painted on the wall. Although this is supposed to be a new locale, it can clearly be seen from the preceding frame that it is shot approximately 20 feet to the rear and left of the last setting. Iris in on Caligari's caravan; it is painted in flowing stripes and patches and leans somewhat to the right. One wheel is partially visible on left and a short flight of steps leads up to the door in the centre of the end which is visible; to the right of the door is a small slanting window. Caligari emerges from the door, descends the steps and goes to peer round his caravan, first on one side, then on the other. Looking about him expectantly, he returns and pauses briefly in front of the door, then darts into the caravan and swiftly closes the door behind him. Iris out.

TITLE : *On the way home.*

Resume on the street setting in which we last saw Alan, Francis and Jane, though the camera has now moved slightly to the right. Francis and Alan enter from left and saunter towards camera. They stop in the shadow of a dark form on the left and begin to talk. Francis makes as though to ascend the stairs.
Francis, who has now begun to climb the stairs, speaks over his shoulder to Alan, who has a bemused expression on his face.

TITLE : ' *Alan, we both love her.*'

The faces of the two friends are brightly lit by a street lamp hanging above them. They both look full of good intentions, fully determined to behave as nobly as possible in this difficult situation.

TITLE : ' *We must let her choose. But whatever her choice, we shall always remain friends.*'

They grip each other's hand firmly in their determination to be fair-minded.
Francis disappears up the flight of stairs on the left, while Alan turns and walks away in the opposite direction, his coat billowing around him. Iris out on the street lamp.

TITLE : *Night.*

We are back in Alan's room; the bed is in centre of frame, parallel to the right wall which is painted with black and white designs. In the background is one of the ladder-back chairs, strongly lit. Alan is asleep, his head high on the pillow, face upturned. A sinister-looking shadow slowly begins to creep across Alan and up on to the wall, assuming the outline of a human form greatly magnified. Alan suddenly awakes, utterly terrified as the person we cannot see slowly approaches his bed. He waves his hands about in front of him in a hysterical and fruitless attempt to fend the approaching person off.

55

Close-up of two hands with their fingers extended.

Alan is now sitting bolt upright in bed, threshing about wildly in total panic. On the wall is the shadow of a hand with a knife poised above his head.

Alan stares, his mouth open; he clutches at his throat in a feeble attempt to defend himself.

The shadow on the wall raises the stiletto to strike and we see the shadow of Alan's hands raised to ward off the expected attack before the two close together in a desperate struggle. The standing shadow seizes the wrists of Alan's shadow, then raises the stiletto again and plunges downward. (Production still on page 40)

A woman dressed in black comes hurrying down the alley between two houses at the rear of the street scene outside the house where Francis lives, almost colliding with two men who pass in front of her. Her hurrying manner suggests profound emotional disturbance and shock, as she goes towards the stairs at left and begins to dart rapidly up them. (Still on page 40)

Francis is in his room standing by the large leather sofa; he is carefully adjusting his bow-tie. The woman in black rushes into the room behind Francis, who abruptly spins round to discover the cause of this sudden intrusion. The woman moves towards him, her face registering extreme grief and horror. (Still on page 57)

TITLE: '*Mr. Francis! Mr. Francis! Mr. Alan is dead. Murdered.*'

The woman is speaking passionately, her left hand clasped to her breast. Francis's hands are still raised at the horrible news, his face expresses a mixture of sorrow and disbelief. The woman turns away to hide her face in her hands, completely overcome by her grief. Francis holds his fingertips almost together; his mouth has fallen partly open and he stares blankly away. He turns to the woman, who looks up startled, and points to the rear of the room. They both begin to move back past the sofa in the direction in which Francis has pointed.

In Alan's room, his disordered bed bears witness to the recent struggle, though we cannot see Alan's body from this angle. Francis and the woman rush into the room. He gazes horror-struck in the direction of the bed, before moving towards it; the woman looks

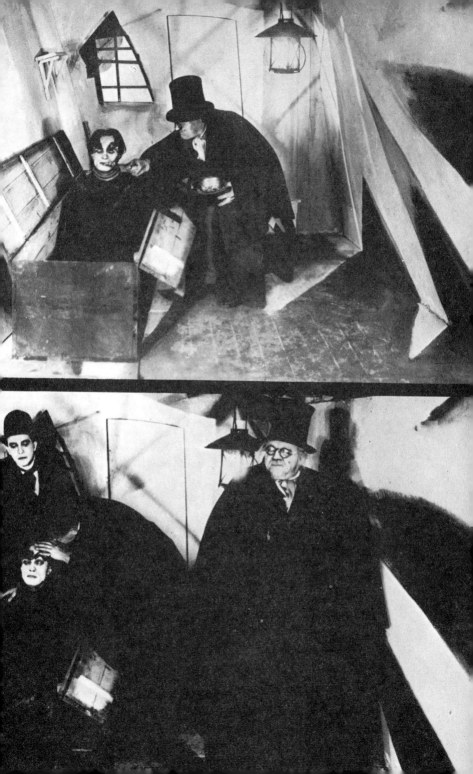

away. Francis turns and comes slowly towards camera, eyes switching from left to right; the woman remains in the background by the window. A look of comprehension, which brings on a fit of gasping and swallowing, suddenly flits across Francis's face as he recalls something.

TITLE : ' *The prophecy of the somnambulist!* '

Francis stands staring, wide-eyed, trying to grasp an idea which his mind cannot quite entertain. The woman is almost lost in shadow at the rear of the room. Francis raises the finger of his left hand to his cheek; his expression is that of a man engaged in the solution of a terrible problem. Iris out.

Diamond iris in, widening to reveal a staircase curving left and losing itself in shadow. Francis enters right, arms waving, and disappears at a run up the staircase.

Francis rushes into an office in the police-station. There is a table in the centre of the office and two policemen are perched on very high stools, one on either side of the table. A number of papers are strewn on the floor in the foreground. On the left is a range of pigeon-holes from which more papers protrude; there is a triangular window in the back wall, on which a number of triangular shapes are painted. Both policemen are crouching conscientiously over their work when Francis enters, but his precipitous entrance causes them to climb down from their stools and close round him. They are both wearing flat round hats with chin straps and long jackets with double rows of shiny buttons. Francis clutches the arm of one of them.

Francis, very close to hysteria, has now laid a hand on both policemen, whose looks betray extreme concern as Francis talks wildly, eyes staring and chin thrust forward. He removes a hand from one of the policemen and raises it to the back of his neck, then slowly pantomimes the stabbing; he gasps and pants as he thrusts upwards and downwards. The two policemen lean back slightly and exchange a meaningful glance behind his back. Francis's arm remains upraised in a gesture of determination.

TITLE : ' *I will not rest until I have got to the bottom of these terrible events.*'

65

Francis, eyes rolling dramatically, stands with arm aloft.

One of the policemen dashes off left, while the other remains with Francis, who has now started to make stabbing motions again. The other policeman re-enters, closely followed by a youngish inspector wearing a short cape and a high conical hat. The three policemen all cluster round Francis, who stands at the front of the group with his right arm raised. The inspector confers with his two subordinates behind Francis.

Francis descends the stairs from the police station slowly and hesitantly; he is still very dazed and bewildered by events. At the foot of the stairs, where low-angle lighting gives his face a macabre pallor, he comes towards camera, then stops and raises his hand wearily to his brow. He pushes his hair back, then lets his arm slowly fall over his face, before leaving right, head bowed. Iris out. The scene changes to that of a peaceful garden. On the left is a high wall which curves gently to centre rear and immediately beneath it is a path which runs along the length of the wall. On the right of the path are a number of cutouts representing trees and bushes. Jane, dressed in a flowing white gown, comes down the few steps which lead from a doorway in the wall and hurries along the path to meet Francis who is advancing towards her. When they meet, the girl catches hold of his arm and turns to walk with him along the path. Francis is staggering slightly from the effect of recent events. They stop near the doorway and the girl gazes up into his face, trying to divine the reason for his disturbed condition. Jane has to bend slightly forward to look into Francis's face, but as Francis reveals the reason for his grief, she straightens up suddenly, eyes dilated with horror. Francis slumps left and sinks down on a bench by the wall; shoulders bowed, he is the picture of utter wretchedness. The girl asks him to tell her more of what has happened; every detail that Francis adds to his story draws a further shudder of horror from her, until, unable to bear any more, she turns away again, incapable of containing her grief. (Still on page 57)

Jane enters a sitting room, the sides of which are curtained with broad swathes of scrim. In the centre of the room is a small occasional table on which there is a vase containing three unnatural looking flowers; there is a long curved sofa behind the table; the rear wall is painted with a scallop pattern. Jane is followed in almost immediately by Francis and they both come to the centre of the room, standing between the table and sofa, where the girl motions to Francis to remain before leaving the room. Francis stands alone for a few seconds by the table and then an older man, Jane's father, very carefully dressed in dark suit and high white collar, enters and goes swiftly towards the table to talk to Francis.

Dissolve to Francis and Jane's father talking together. As Francis talks he gestures downwards with his clenched fist; the other man, a very serious expression on his face, listens carefully, looking over his spectacles at Francis. He appears very concerned about what he hears but he manages all the same to lay a reassuring hand on Francis's wrist.

TITLE : ' *I will get a permit from the police to examine the somnambulist.*'

Jane's father continues talking animatedly while Francis listens intently. He nods in agreement as the other man points off left across him before they both leave the room.

Night has fallen; we see a narrow street in the town, partly illuminated by a bright lamp which is suspended above the street. The walls of the houses on either side of the street lean crazily in all directions; there are slanting windows in the walls on right and a shadowy doorway in the wall opposite. The figure of a man emerges furtively from the shadows at rear and moves cautiously forward, hugging the wall on right and remaining well concealed in its shadow. His features and dress gradually become more visible as he moves towards camera and we see that he has a full black beard. He is wearing a dark jacket and sweater, with trousers in a lighter material tucked into knee boots. He moves, still furtive, out of the shadow and crosses to the other side of the street, constantly glancing over his shoulder to make sure he is still unobserved. (Still on page 58) Then, with a last swift movement, he darts into the doorway on left. Iris out.

Iris in, upper left of screen, on a woman wearing a frilly night cap shouting and screaming at a window.

Title : ' *Murder! ...Help! ...Murder!* '

The woman screams frantically from the window.

The bearded man suddenly rushes out of the doorway and into the street, now seen in high angle shot. A knife glints in his hand as he rushes down the street in the direction from which he came. Suddenly, however, he is forced to turn round as a group of towns-people, attracted by the woman's cries, rush into the street. The man turns and comes towards camera, one eye on his pursuers and his knife raised defensively in front of him.

The bearded man is finally captured by his pursuers in another street — the one from which the flight of steps lead up to Francis's room. The man struggles so violently that several townspeople are needed to hold him down; they manage after a struggle to drag him away. Iris out. (Still on page 58)

Iris in on Caligari, dressed in his top hat and long dark coat; he is bending low over something and making vigorous stirring motions. Iris widens to reveal the interior of Caligari's caravan and Caligari stirring a bowl of porridge or similar mashed food. The interior is almost entirely bare of furnishing or decoration; behind Caligari is the end of the caravan with the door which we have already seen from the outside; to the left of the door is a small window. There is a long chest on left which can be recognised as the cabinet in which Cesare has been displayed at the fair; it is now lying length-ways. By the cabinet is a low table on which Caligari sits while he stirs the mashed food. Caligari rises to his feet, still stirring, walks around the back of the table and places the bowl of food on it. He turns to the cabinet and opens the doors to disclose Cesare lying absolutely prone and stiff, seemingly in a very deep sleep. Caligari goes round to the head of the cabinet, reaches in, places both hands under Cesare's arms and raises him to a sitting position; Cesare's eyes are still closed. Caligari steadies the somnambulist in his sitting position as Cesare looks as though he may very well fall back into the cabinet. The Doctor turns and picks up the bowl of food he has prepared and begins to feed the mash to Cesare, stirring the food between each spoonful. (Still on page 59)

The scene changes to the outside of Caligari's caravan. Francis, followed by Jane's father, comes in from left. Francis is wearing a flowing cape and a hat with a rounded crown and brim; his companion is wearing a top hat. They go towards the door of the caravan and Francis moves slightly to the right so that he can look through the window before knocking on the door.

Inside the caravan, Caligari, who is still feeding Cesare, looks up suddenly as he hears the knocking on his door. He hurriedly puts the bowl down and pushes Cesare back into a recumbent position in the cabinet and quickly closes the doors. He goes towards the door, but before he opens it, he crouches slightly and turns to take one last look at the interior to make certain everything is in order. He finally moves to open the door.

Francis and Jane's father are still waiting outside the caravan; Francis knocks urgently at the door. Caligari opens the door and sticks his head out to look at Francis; the other man is excluded from his view because the door opens outwards. Francis and Caligari exchange some words which seem to make the latter very excited, for he suddenly jumps down the steps, slams the door shut behind him and spreads out his arms to bar the two men from entering the caravan.

Caligari continues to bar the way of the others into his caravan, glaring implacably at them through his round spectacles, shouting 'Nein!' in reply to their entreaties to enter. The Doctor produces a piece of paper from his pocket which he shows to Caligari, provoking Caligari to clench his fists in fury and further shouts of 'Nein!' After further exchanges Caligari finally relents, shuffles slightly forward, then turns and bows towards the caravan with exaggerated politeness for Jane's father to enter; he goes in, followed by Francis and Caligari.

The stairs leading to the police station; four townspeople enter dragging the bearded man, whom they half pull, half push up the stairs. A curl of smoke, whose existence is unexplained, rises from left.

Three policemen in uniform are sitting round the table in the station office; two are on high stools on either side of the table and the other is sitting lower down behind the table. The group of men from the town enter at a run, propelling their bearded captive into the room. The policemen climb down from their stools and join the townspeople in the centre of the room around the criminal. The townsmen, all of whom are wearing capes and conical hats, point accusingly at the man they have captured.

Camera pans over the faces of the men as they all try to give their evidence simultaneously. They talk rapidly, excitedly.

The captive has a hang-dog, beaten look in the middle of his accusers.

Close-up of the criminal, hair disordered and chin covered with several days stubble. He glares balefully at his captors. On the right the face of a townsman is visible, serious, slightly worried.

One of the men hands the knife which has been confiscated from the criminal to the inspector. The latter balances it thoughtfully in his hand, looks at the criminal and gestures left, whereupon the policemen seize the captive and march him firmly off. The four men from the town remain with the inspector; the man closest to him points to the knife and speaks and the others move closer to offer their opinion before finally leaving in a group. The Inspector remains gazing at the knife and then turns and goes back to the desk behind him.

Meanwhile, inside Caligari's caravan, Jane's father, a doctor, is examining Cesare who has been raised to a half-sitting position. Caligari is standing right, fuming with rage, while Francis has taken up a position at the head of the cabinet to see what Jane's father is doing. (Still on page 59) The doctor looks up and glances towards Caligari, before bending again to listen to Cesare's heartbeat. Cesare's eyes are still closed.

Caligari slides his eyes craftily to left, followed by a movement of his head. Then slowly he moves his head and eyes back right.

Jane's father straightens up and turns towards Caligari, speaking sharply to him and gesturing with both hands.

TITLE : ' *Wake him up.*'

Caligari scowls malevolently at the doctor and firmly refuses to carry out his request. Francis looks through the window, his attention suddenly attracted by something outside. He dashes to the door and disappears through it.

Outside Caligari's caravan; Francis bursts suddenly out of the door as another man enters scene and promptly leaves again after handing Francis a handbill, which Francis starts reading avidly. He turns and calls to Jane's father, who in turn comes dashing down the steps to read the handbill; the two men stand bent over the document.

INSERT:

> *LATE EXTRA!*
> *HOLSTENWALL MURDER*
> *MYSTERY SOLVED.*
> *The killer of two recent victims*
> *has been caught in his third*
> *attempt.*

Francis and the doctor look closely at the document, then turn and look over their shoulders as Caligari comes abruptly through his front door. They leave hurriedly left and Caligari, standing on the steps of his caravan with his hat in his hand, makes two exaggeratedly sweeping bows after their departing figures. He grins slyly, then raises his hat to his face and peeps over it. He cackles gaily, replaces the hat firmly on his head and goes back into the caravan, turning momentarily to look in the direction which Francis and his companion have taken.

TITLE: *Worried by her father's long absence . . .*

Jane is sitting at the small table in the scrim-hung room in her house. She is gazing abstractedly at an open book which she holds chest-high in front of her. She turns her head to look left — anxiously, as though waiting for someone — then turns back to her book again. Finally she shuts the book with a gesture of impatience, rises, looks around worriedly and makes as though to leave the room.

In the meantime, Francis and her father have arrived at the police station. The bearded criminal is standing between two policemen, scowling horribly. Jane's father is sitting on the right of the room on a ladder-back chair and Francis stands just behind him, his elbow resting on the back of the chair.

Francis's face is very pale, registering deep anguish.

Everyone is staring intently at the criminal, whose bearded face shifts uneasily.

The criminal looks shiftily to one side and speaks through gritted teeth. His eyes move from side to side as he infuses greater vehemence into what he is saying.

TITLE : ' *I had nothing to do with the first two murders, so help me God.*'

The expression on the speaker's face becomes slightly calmer.

Jane's father barks something at the criminal, moving his head up and down emphatically. The latter stares in front of him, head slightly bent.

Close-up of the criminal as he continues his account.

TITLE : ' *The old woman . . . yes; it's true I wanted to kill her . . . with a stab from the same kind of dagger, so as to throw suspicion on to the mystery murderer.*'

The criminal begins to speak very emphatically.

Jane's father and Francis listen intently as the criminal finishes his account.

Puzzlement registers on the faces of Jane's father and Francis. The doctor looks upwards over his spectacles and Francis looks down at the doctor, before looking again in the direction of the criminal.

Francis turns away from the criminal towards the camera, puts his hand to his brow and leans on the back of the doctor's chair. His expression shows that he does not know what to believe; iris out upper right on his head and hand.

Iris in on the roundabout in the upper right of the fairground scene; the roundabout is no longer turning. Iris also includes Jane's face. The iris widens as Jane turns to look over her left shoulder, before walking across the open space in front of the roundabout and the railings which mark the top of the flight of steps. She is now wearing a long dress made of striped material. She walks towards the rear of the open space, then turns and looks around her. Finally she crosses to the head of the steps on the right and goes down them, serpenting from one side to the other as she descends the various flights and finally disappears from view.

Jane comes towards camera down the alleyway between the fairground tents and marquees. On the right is the platform in front of Caligari's tent, with the unrolled poster of Cesare still in position. Jane advances cautiously down the alleyway, peering about her. When she reaches Caligari's tent, she first gazes at the poster, then begins to mount the steps to the platform. There is some trepidation in her attitude, but she is determined to go on in spite of herself.

Caligari's head pokes out of the tent opening. He looks to right and left, glaring through his spectacles.

Jane, who has now reached the top of the short flight of stairs leading on to the platform, recoils slightly at the unnerving sight of the doctor, now leaning forward out of the tent opening and gesturing towards her with the head of his cane.

Jane's face in close-up looks deadly pale, an effect accentuated by the dark shadow around the eyes, which now register alarm at the sudden apparition of Caligari.

Caligari comes completely out of the tent opening to speak to Jane; he is still gesturing towards her with his cane. She leans forward to speak to him from her position at the top of the stairs and he bends down to her level to hear more clearly.

TITLE : *Is my father here — the doctor?*

Caligari smiles as Jane speaks to him, almost as though he were making a special effort to be polite to her. He shakes his head. A crafty grin flits across Caligari's face and he looks away right. Then his eyes switch back left; he looks extremely pleased with himself.

TITLE : *' Oh yes — the doctor. Won't you come in and wait for him?'*

As Caligari replies, Jane, still very ill at ease in the presence of this bizarre individual, raises her hands across her chest and draws back. Caligari gestures towards the tent opening, inviting her to come in. (Production still on page 60) Her hesitancy shows clearly and Caligari's bowing and cajoling become more frenetic. Eventually

73

she steps forward reluctantly on to the platform and Caligari disappears inside the tent though his hand is still visible beckoning from the opening.

Inside the tent, Caligari enters left, followed by Jane to whom he turns with a sinister smile, beckoning her to come forward as he moves towards the cabinet now standing in its former position, upright on the tiny stage at the rear of the tent. Jane looks extremely apprehensive as Caligari uses all his gifts as a showman to increase the feeling of tension in the situation. Standing to the left of the cabinet, he extends his forefinger and flips open first one, then the other door of the cabinet, revealing Cesare standing motionless, eyes closed. Caligari hops into a half crouch and springs round, grinning unpleasantly, to see what effect this revelation has had on Jane.

Caligari's eyes stare wickedly and brightly through his round spectacles.

Jane draws away from the sinister form of Cesare, but Caligari gestures with his hand for her to come nearer and points jerkily towards Cesare with the head of his cane. Jane moves slowly towards the still figure of the somnambulist, fascinated in spite of herself. She moves to the right of the cabinet and looks upwards towards the occupant making her face almost invisible. Cesare suddenly inclines his head slightly towards the girl, opens his eyes and glares at her. (Still on page 60) Jane is terrified; she backs away away and turns, raising her hand to her throat. Caligari looks on, very satisfied with the effect of his little exhibition. Jane, overcome with terror, screams and rushes away. Caligari and Cesare move their heads slightly to follow her departure. Iris out on Caligari's face.

TITLE : *After the funeral.*

Iris in on the cemetery wall which runs from right foreground to a half-grill gate at rear. Foliage forms are painted on the wall and branch and leaf forms hang down from above. Jane, her father and Francis enter through the gate and walk forwards towards camera. They are all dressed in mourning and Jane walks with her head slightly bowed. The trio walks solemnly forward and disappears on

74

right. Iris out.

TITLE : *Night.*

Francis has returned to the fairground, where we see him descending the steps behind the railing of the balustrade, gradually disappearing from view as he negotiates each successive flight.

Francis enters the alleyway between the tents and marquees from the rear. He runs forward quickly yet stealthily, keeping close to the tents on the left, the opposite side to Caligari's tent. When he reaches a point immediately opposite Caligari's tent, he tries to peer through the opening, then swiftly darts across the alleyway to the foot of the platform to get a closer look. Still not satisfied, he pulls himself up on to the platform and creeps forward on his hands and knees to the entrance of the tent. He raises the flap slightly and looks inside, finally pushing his head completely through the opening. Then, seemingly worried that someone should see him in this strange posture, he looks furtively behind him. Not seeing what he was looking for, he gets up and goes off down the alleyway, still hesitant, still looking for something.

Francis enters from the left outside Caligari's caravan and runs crouching across to the right where he sidles up to the window.

Francis peers curiously through the window of Caligaris' caravan. Through the window Caligari can be seen sitting in a chair on the left, apparently asleep, his hands folded under his chin and supported on the top of his cane. By his side the upper half of the open cabinet is visible, revealing Cesare's upturned face seen from below. He also appears to be asleep.

Francis is still gazing through the window.

Jane's bedroom in medium long shot; at the rear are very high narrow windows with painted scroll work between them. In the foreground is Jane's bed, lavishly draped with white material. Jane is asleep, face upturned and her right arm curling round the back of her head.

At the same time, just outside Jane's house, Cesare advances stealthily down the path by the garden wall, still dressed in his tight dark clothes. He walks, with a strange stiff-legged gait, right arm extended above his head as he feels his way along the wall with his hand. (Still on page 61) He finally comes to a lighted doorway in the wall and he turns slowly and mounts the three steps which lead up to it and disappears.

Jane is still sleeping in the same position as before. Behind one of the windows at the rear of the room the sinister figure of Cesare slowly rises up.

The face and torso of Cesare appear more clearly through the window. A long stiletto gleams in his hand.

Jane, however, continues to sleep peacefully, as Cesare begins to remove a bar from the window.

Cesare has now completely detached the bar from the window; he quickly tosses it away and steps over the window sill into the room. Cesare moves away slowly from the window, gliding towards the bed like some graceful automaton. As he comes to the edge of the bed, he raises the shining stiletto over the sleeping form of the oblivious Jane. The whites of his eyes are brightly visible.

Cesare stares forward, expressionless, the long dagger poised for the downward plunge.

Cesare begins to stab downwards towards Jane's body. Then suddenly he stops and his shoulders move jerkily several times.

An almost benevolent expression spreads over his face, as he drops the knife and begins to bend forward slowly again.

Gently, Cesare bends down towards Jane, slowly extending his fingers and reaching out with his right arm until it touches the hair of the sleeping girl. (Still on page 61) Jane wakes up immediately, absolutely beside herself with terror. Cesare seizes her wrists.

Grinning grotesquely, Cesare struggles with the girl's wrists and pulls her face towards him. She holds her eyes tightly shut. Cesare, laughing, grasps her by her chin and hair and pushes her down on the bed, where she continues to struggle.

Jane fights with Cesare on the bed and manages to roll away from him for an instant, but then he manages to grasp both wrists again as she hurls herself forward in a determined effort to shake him off. In an effort to hold her still, Cesare wraps his arm round the girl's breast, whereupon she raises her hands as though to scratch his face, so that he is forced to grab her wrists again. Finally Cesare manages to get both his hands round the girl's neck.

Cesare picks Jane up, his left arm passing round her waist. She is still struggling so violently that Cesare is unable to detach her from a bundle of bedclothes which he picks up with her.

Two men are asleep in medium shot, heads pointing towards the centre of the frame. They suddenly sit up in bed, looking very alarmed, and point off left. The older man turns to the younger and they both begin to get out of bed as quickly as possible.

Cesare, in the meantime, has grasped the girl more firmly and is carrying her towards the window through which he entered; the bedclothes fall to the floor as Jane still struggles faintly under his arm.

The two men, now risen from their beds, move away from camera into darkness.

The two men rush into Jane's bedroom from the rear and dash towards the empty bed, waving their arms in consternation and confusion. A dark-haired woman, wearing a white blouse and dark skirt, runs in after them. Another man follows her into the room, pushes his way between the two others and throws himself on the rumpled bed in a burst of grief and desperation. Then the first two men and the woman notice the window open at the back of the room and all three run back towards it.

The younger man points up through the window towards the rooftops. His companion looks through the window in the same direction.

The man who prostrated himself on the bed now picks himself up and goes to join the other three at the window.

He rudely pushes the woman out of his way in his anxiety to look out of the window.

Cesare comes from the left carrying the girl bundled under his arm; he makes his way across very precipitous rooftops which lean towards each other at crazy angles. Long narrow chimney-pots pointing in all directions, stand out against a brightly-lit sky. Cesare walks swiftly along the ridge of one of the rooftops and then begins to disappear from sight behind the crest of a roof. (Original design for this set and still on page 62)

Caligari, seen through the bars of his caravan window, is still apparently asleep, hands folded on top of his cane. By his side, the figure of Cesare is still lying in the open cabinet.

Outside the caravan, Francis gazes intently through the window. Cesare, still carrying Jane, comes out of the brightly lit doorway in the garden wall. (Still on page 63) He moves away quickly down the path towards the rear, keeping close to the wall. A second or two later, the young man, who has already been seen in the bedroom, starts out of the doorway in hot pursuit of Cesare; he is followed closely by the older man, still wearing pyjama trousers. They run quickly down the path and disappear.

Cesare, now staggering under his human burden, is approaching the crown of a small hump-backed bridge, from which a tortuous path leads down. The bridge is very abruptly arched and lamps and a balustrade are painted along its parapet. In the foreground are a number of gaunt gothic tree forms, giving a sinister air to the scene. The sides of the screen are blacked out. Cesare staggers down the path from the crown of the bridge, turning his feet outwards in an effort to preserve his balance. (Still on page 63) As he comes down from the bridge, his two pursuers appear on the path on the other side of the bridge, rapidly gaining on him. Cesare lets Jane fall to the ground and runs away down the path. (Still on page 64) The two leading men pick up her prostrate body and, joined by a third, carry her back up the path and over the bridge. As they pick her up, a number of men dash past them to continue the pursuit of Cesare.

Cesare appears climbing up a steeply sloping path on a hillside covered with coarse, spear-pointed grass. On the horizon are cut-out tree forms with weird tapering branches; they stand out in silhouette against a brightly-lit sky. As he mounts the path, Cesare shows all the signs of great exhaustion : his shoulders are sagging, his arms are droopingly outstretched, as though he is making a feeble attempt to retain his balance. He staggers, stops, turns, crumples to the ground and rolls away out of sight down the hillside.

Francis is still standing looking through the window of Caligari's caravan. He turns away slightly from the window and half-faces camera; he seems pensive, troubled.

He ducks away from the window and moves stealthily away; he

comes towards camera and exits centre foreground.

Jane lies sprawled in a chair in the sitting room of her father's house. Her father, the doctor, is bending anxiously over her. A maidservant leaves the room at rear as Francis rushes in from the left and throws himself passionately at Jane's feet, imploring her to show some sign of consciousness. (Still on page 81)

Dissolve to Francis and the doctor lifting Jane into an upright sitting position. Her eyes, though open, are quite expressionless and the iris is almost completely surrounded by white. Francis gazes imploringly into the eyes of his beloved. (Still on page 81) Jane at last begins to look around her with signs of increasing consciousness; but the muscles of her face freeze as a terrible memory recurs to her.

TITLE : ' *Cesare . . .*'

Jane shrieks again and raises her hands to her face. Francis shakes his head negatively, almost pityingly, as he looks up into her terror-stricken face. Jane nods her head again, very certain she is correct about her attacker's identity. Francis, a worried expression on his face, rises to his feet and joins Jane's father standing behind his daughter's chair. He takes the doctor's hand and places it emphatically on his chest.

TITLE : ' *It can't have been Cesare. Cesare was asleep all the time. I have been watching him for hours.*'

Francis emphasises what he has just said with a firm gesture of his clenched hand. Jane, for her part, raises both hands and clenches her fists, absolutely convinced she is right. The doctor bends forward to listen intently to his daughter. Then he turns to look at Francis, who remains equally firmly convinced by what he believes to be the evidence of his own eyes.

The doctor bends down to listen to what Jane has to say. She half-turns her head to the left and raises it slightly towards her father. Iris out.

Back at the police-station; two policemen sit one on either side of the central table. Francis dashes in from the left and stops in front of the table, turning to the policeman at left with an excited movement. The policeman climbs down from his stool, as does his companion. All three men turn towards camera and Francis, now talking excitedly and looking wildly about him, emphasises his words with downward strokes of his right hand. He is beginning to appear tired now, as though recent events are proving too much for him. He raises his hand to his brow and stares hard at the policeman on the left before speaking.

TITLE : ' *Is the prisoner safely in his cell?* '

Francis looks at the one on the left who nods affirmatively, as does his colleague. Francis looks utterly bewildered.

TITLE : ' *I should like to see him.* '

The two policemen confer briefly between themselves, then lead Francis away between them.

Francis comes down the station stairs followed by the two policemen; the three exit at left. Iris out.

Iris opens out to reveal an enclosed space with large inverted pyramidal forms on either side, representing the outside of the gaol. A figure ' 5 ' is printed boldly on the form at left. The policemen enter from the shadows at the rear of the space, followed at a distance by Francis. He follows them as they walk round the form, beckoning him to come and look at something with them.

The two policemen and Francis in close-up look right. The policemen are in profile, while Francis has turned away from camera. The policemen's faces, very solemn, are strongly lit from below; one of them has a sweeping handle-bar moustache, the other a tiny tooth-brush affair.

The bearded criminal is squatting on the floor of his cell in the centre of a white painted patch in the form of four trapezoids splayed out star-fashion. Behind him the wall is painted in broad irregular bands of white and black; there is a distorted window high in the wall behind him. His right leg is attached by a length of chain with massive links to an irregular block at left. The criminal raises his head, then slowly lets it sink down on his chest again. (Still on page 82)

Francis turns from the triangular-shaped peep-hole, through which

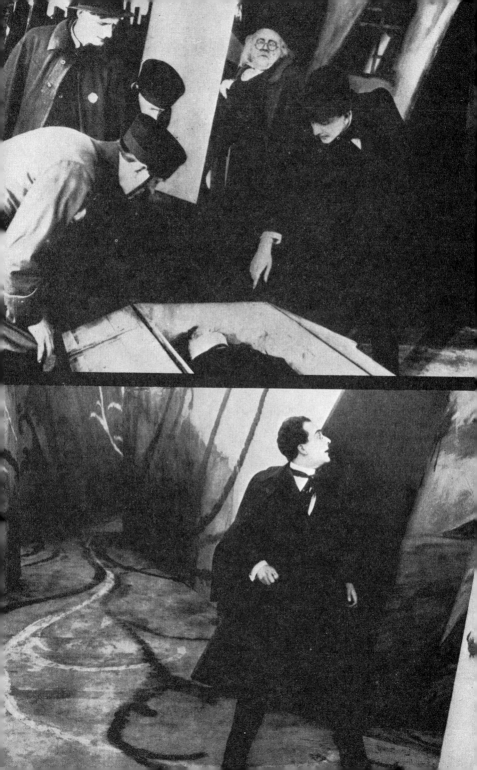

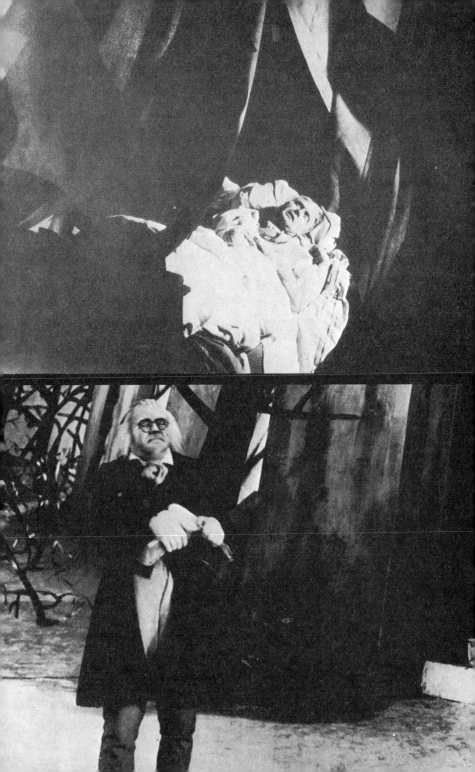

he has been looking at the criminal, to look at the policemen. Then he turns to face camera, his face drawn and worried — is there nothing stable or fixed in the world?

Back at Caligari's caravan, Cesare's master is looking anxiously through the bars of his window. His eyes shift backwards and forwards uneasily as he anxiously awaits the return of the somnambulist.

Caligari is apparently asleep again in the chair by the open cabinet, in which the recumbent form of Cesare is still visible.

Outside the caravan, Francis enters from left and goes towards the window, closely followed by the inspector and two policemen.

Caligari can still be seen through the window sitting beside Cesare's cabinet.

The policemen hesitate briefly in front of the caravan door and the inspector turns towards his two subordinates. Francis has taken up his old post by the window. The inspector motions to the two policemen to position themselves on either side of the caravan, while he raps sharply on the door. Caligari, fully dressed in hat and coat and carrying his cane, bounces out angrily, slams the door behind him and looks defiantly at the inspector.*

Caligari makes forbidding gestures with his cane, firmly resisting all attempts to enter his caravan. The inspector steps quickly up from the left and shoves Caligari roughly inside.

The inspector pushes Caligari to the right of the door which he then opens, whereupon the two policemen climb up the steps and enter the caravan.

Caligari looks out of the corner of his eyes towards the open door, then he closes his eyes and allows his head to fall slowly forward. His right hand is clasped to his chest.

The policemen come out of the caravan and descend the steps carrying the notorious cabinet between them. They set it down on the ground and the inspector and Francis start forward expectantly.

Caligari rolls his eyes in panic as he looks downward towards the box. He raises his clenched fist to his face and draws back.

---

* In the Museum of Modern Art print of the film there is a title inserted at this point: '*He must not be disturbed*', which did not appear in the National Film Archive print.

The two policemen stand back and the inspector quickly bends forward and opens the lid of the cabinet. None of the men can contain his curiosity and they all bend over the box to look at the figure of Cesare which lies revealed. (Still on page 83)

The head of Cesare is seen from below the chin; below the chin is the high neck of the polo neck sweater.

Francis bends forward to grasp the figure in the box by the shoulders. Behind him, Caligari, wide-eyed with alarm, raises his hands in horror. He is not so paralysed by the situation, however, that he cannot make good his escape while all the other men are preoccupied with the figure in the box. Francis pulls the figure up to its full length, then flings it down disgustedly on the box as he realises he is holding a dummy.

Caligari appears running up a sloping path across a hillside very similar to the one on which Cesare collapsed. It is also painted with jagged lines to represent spearhead grass and there are the same gaunt silhouettes of trees on the ridge of the hill. Caligari runs up the path to the top of the hill, where he pauses briefly — a sinister cloaked and hatted figure silhouetted against the bright sky — before disappearing from view over the crest. As he drops from sight, Francis appears on the path in the foreground and also dashes up to the crest of the hill before disappearing on the other side in pursuit of the fugitive.

Caligari appears running over the small hump-backed bridge and down the tortuous path where Cesare earlier let Jane fall; he sways wildly as he comes at a strange shuffling run towards camera. The dark figure of Francis materialises on the crown of the bridge, in hot pursuit. He chases Caligari out in centre foreground.

Caligari runs up from right along another path up a steep hillside. The scene is very similar to the one in which Caligari has already crossed a hillside, but the path he follows is broader and there are fewer tree silhouettes on the crest of the hill. Francis follows Caligari closely up the path, gaining on him steadily.

Caligari scuttles in at right of a street scene, which is brightly illuminated from above by street lamps. The walls on either side of the street disappear into shadow; a poster stands out prominently on one of the walls. Caligari runs towards a gate at the rear which he opens and through which he disappears. Francis enters right, pauses by the corner of the wall to peer round it, then begins to move swiftly towards the gate through which Caligari has disappeared.

But before Francis reaches the gate his attention is caught by the poster which is prominently displayed on one of the walls. He stops to read it; we note that there is a tiny arrow pointing from it towards the gate through which Caligari has just passed. Francis starts back as he reads what is written.

Title : (*LUNATIC ASYLUM*)

Francis shrinks back from the poster, then turns towards the gate and opens it gingerly.

Francis is escorted into a courtyard by a white-jacketed attendant. At the rear of the courtyard is the light-coloured facade of the main building of the Institution, in which there are three large rounded arches with vaguely oriental patterns painted round them. About eight feet above these, set in the wall of the facade, is a row of eight smaller arched openings. The courtyard itself is painted with alternate rays of light and dark which spread out from a radial point close to the centre of the yard. On the right of the courtyard a number of deep leather armchairs are set out. After escorting Francis to the centre of the yard, the attendant walks swiftly to the arch on right of the facade and disappears. Francis remains in the courtyard gazing inquisitively about him. The attendant returns from the archway accompanied by a youngish doctor wearing a long white coat. The two men approach Francis and the doctor remains to talk to him, while the attendant goes out past the leather armchairs on the right.

Francis speaks excitedly to the young doctor.

Title : ' *Have you a patient here named Dr. Caligari?* '

The doctor shakes his head negatively and Francis becomes more frantic, moving his hands excitedly to emphasise his words. The young doctor turns and goes back towards the arch where an older man, grey-haired and also wearing a long white coat, has appeared. The two doctors confer briefly together, while Francis remains in foreground, back to camera. The two men walk forward to join Francis and the older one listens carefully to Francis's story, a worried expression on his face. Francis, for his part, looks very puzzled and distressed.

TITLE : *' The Director came back only today. Perhaps you would like to talk to him yourself? '*

Francis nods, signifying that he would like to see the Director, and he turns to follow the older doctor through the archway. The younger man digs his hands deeply into the pockets of his white coat and goes out right.

The old doctor appears on the left leading Francis down a hallway towards a door on right. The floor of the hallway is painted with black tendril forms. The doctor turns to Francis and opens the door in the wall of the hall and then waits for Francis to precede him through it. Francis removes his hat as he passes through the doorway, while the doctor remains in the hall and closes the door after Francis and turns to retrace his steps down the hall.

Francis enters a strangely chaotic room. The walls are very irregular and painted with curved shapes; the floor is painted with dark wavy lines. There is a standing skeleton on left and at rear of room is a large irregularly curved desk. In front of the desk are several high piles of books and there are a further two piles on the desk. Between these two piles can be seen the bent head of the Director as he works at his desk; we can see that he has white straggling hair. Francis advances slowly towards him.

Behind the head of the Director is the heavily upholstered leather back of his armchair. Slowly the Director raises his head to reveal the madly staring eyes, round spectacles and long white hair of Dr. Caligari.

Francis, unable to control his shock, stumbles over one of the piles of books, then starts backwards under the basilisk gaze of Caligari. He spins round as quickly as he can and flees to the door.

Francis backs out through the door into the hall, staring wildly into the room he has just left. (Still on page 83) He manages, however, to gather himself together sufficiently to slam the door shut before lurching unsteadily away down the hall.

Still staggering, Francis appears coming down a flight of stairs and through the central arch of the facade into the courtyard. Three men in white coats rush after him through the arch and together half lift him, half drag him, into one of the leather armchairs on right of the courtyard.

Francis's face has turned a chalky-white with shock and contrasts sharply with the more normal flesh tones of the faces of the three doctors who gather in a semi-circle round his chair, bending forward eagerly to catch his words; they exchange concerned glances. Francis speaks rapidly, turning from one to another of the men.

TITLE: *He — he alone and none other — is Caligari.*

The three doctors look at one another, then bend forward towards Francis, listening intently. Francis talks on, clasping his hands together, imploring them to believe him. He raises his hands to his brow in utter despair at their apparent disbelief. Fade out.

TITLE: *While the Doctor is asleep at his house, investigations are made.*

High angle shot of a man lying asleep on a brightly lit bed; the room around the bed is partly lost in shadow. The bedclothes are very disordered and the head of the man tosses uneasily in his sleep, revealing the features of Caligari. (Still on page 84)

Fade into an exterior scene: Francis is just approaching a door in an outside wall of the Institution. A winding path leads away towards rear past a silhouette tree with thorny branches. As Francis reaches the door, a doctor dressed in a long coat comes out. He stops and speaks to Francis who seems about to push his way past the man and go through the door.

TITLE: ' *He is asleep.*'

The doctor and Francis move away from the door and walk away from camera down the winding path.

Francis and three doctors in long white coats come down the hall towards the door of the Director's office. One of the men opens it and all four disappear inside.

Once inside the Director's office, the four men rush towards the large desk at the rear and begin to examine excitedly the books which are piled on it, looking closely at the titles. The older doctor goes towards the standing skeleton, moves it aside and reaches behind it. The others look on curiously.

Francis and the other two doctors stare intently right.

Behind the skeleton is a small cupboard set deeply in the wall, from which the older man removes two weighty-looking tomes. His triumphant expression plainly shows that he has found what he has been looking for. He opens the first and smiles affirmatively.

The older doctor has rejoined the other three men who are grouped around the desk. Francis opens the upper of the two volumes and the other three gather round to read over his shoulder as he bends forwards over the desk.

INSERT (printed in black-letter type):

Somnambulism.
A Compendium of the University
of Uppsala.
Published in the year 1726.

Francis looks up at the other men, the light of understanding dawning in his eyes.

TITLE : ' *This has always been his special study.*'

Francis looks at the other men, then down at the book again, which he begins to leaf through excitedly, turning the pages with great rapidity.

Caligari, seen from a high angle, is still sleeping restlessly in his disordered bed.

The four men are now bent very closely over one of the pages in the book. Francis's nose is only about a foot from the page.

INSERT (printed in black-letter type):

The Cabinet
of Dr. Caligari
In the year 1703, a mystic by the name of Dr. Caligari, together with a somnambulist called Cesare, used to frequent the fairgrounds ...

90

The doctor on left looks intently at the book over Francis's shoulder. Camera pans right over Francis's face as he reads eagerly.

INSERT (in upper part of screen, the lower third being blacked out; text continues from the preceding insert): *. . . and for months he kept town after town in a state of panic by a series of murders, all of them perpetrated in similar circumstances . . .*

Camera pans from left to right over the men's faces, fascinated by what they read.
The men continued to pore over the same page. Francis traces each line with his right hand as he reads.

INSERT (black-letter type, following on from preceding insert): *. . . for he caused a somnambulist, whom he had entirely subjected to his will, to carry out his fantastic plans. By means of a puppet figure, modelled in the exact likeness of Cesare, which he laid in the chest when Cesare was away, Dr. Caligari was able to allay any suspicion which might fall on the somnambulist.*

Francis leafs swiftly through the rest of the first book, then turns to the second, which is lying on the desk.

INSERT (written in longhand on white; borders of screen are blacked out): *My Diary.*

Francis looks round excitedly at his companions and opens the diary at what must be an important passage, for he immediately crouches over it, chin supported on hands. The other three men gather round again to read over his shoulder.

INSERT (written in longhand on white in the same angular hand as the words ' My Diary ' on the cover; the borders of the screen *March 12th,* left and right are blacked out):
At last — at last! Today I have been notified of the case of a somnambulist.

INSERT (hand-written on white; left and right borders blacked out): *Now I shall be able to prove whether a somnambulist can be compelled to do things of which he knows nothing, things he would never do himself and would abhor doing — whether it is true that one in a trance can be driven to murder.*

Iris in on the four men reading the book in lower half of screen.
Iris in at the same time in upper right half of screen on Caligari
sitting at his desk in the Institution; iris widens to show the whole
of Caligari's office. Caligari's head is once again framed by the two
piles of books on the desk; on the top of the two piles his hands are
tensed, claw-like. A doctor in a long white coat enters from the left
and marches quickly up to Caligari's desk, turning and gesturing
in the direction from which he has just come. Caligari rises im-
periously from his chair, raises an autocratic right hand and
motions to the man, who turns towards camera and advances as
three other doctors, among whom we can recognise the men who
have read Caligari's private books with Francis, wheel a bath-chair
into the room containing Cesare, deadly-pale and slumped to one
side. They stop the bath-chair in the centre of the room; Caligari
struts forward turkey-toed from his desk, hands folded behind his
back. He peers over Cesare and brushes the somnambulist's untidy
hair back from his brow, bending right over him and gazing almost
lovingly into his face. With his other hand he grasps Cesare's wrist
as though to feel his pulse. The four doctors gather round the back
of the chair as Caligari continues to gaze tenderly at the sleeping
form of Cesare. Finally he pulls himself up to his full height, glares
malevolently at the doctors and waves his arms about to dismiss
them; they troop out obediently. After they have left he crouches
over Cesare again, the very picture of solicitous tenderness. Then
he springs upright again, grinning wildly; his head jerks back and
he raises his left arm in a gesture of triumph. He whips round and
dashes back to his desk, picks up a book and begins leafing through
it feverishly. He carries the book towards Cesare, still thumbing
through it violently. He slaps the book when he finds the passage
he wants, puts two fingers on to the page, looks at Cesare again,
flips through a few more pages, then throws his head back,
laughing hysterically. He holds the book high above his head and
rips it in half, still laughing, and drops the torn sections on the
floor and falls on his knees, grasping hold of Cesare's head.
Iris in on Francis and the three doctors poring over Caligari's diary.
Caligari stirs uneasily in his bed; his chest rises and falls heavily as

though he were fighting for breath.

The four men are still engrossed in reading the diary; iris out in lower left of screen.

INSERT (written in longhand on white):
Afternoon.
> *The desire of my life is fulfilled.*
> *Now at last can I unravel the secrets of this Caligari.*

Iris out in lower left of the four men still reading avidly. At the same time iris in in upper right on Caligari facing left, bent over his desk and reading intently. He is wearing a heavy dark coat. Behind him is an untidily arranged pile of books. He rises from his desk and glares towards camera.

TITLE: *In the grip of hallucination.*

Caligari, still standing at his desk, raises his left hand which is bunched like a claw, above his head, then brings it down again behind his back as he turns towards his book. He thrusts his nose between the pages and tucks his left arm behind his back. There is a sudden, puppet-like quality about these movements. He draws himself stiffly upright again, jerking horribly as though in the grip of forces which he cannot control, clutching the book to his chest and staring upward.

TITLE: '*I must know everything . . . I must penetrate into his innermost secrets . . . I must myself become Caligari.*'

Still holding the book tightly under his left arm, Caligari raises his other hand to his brow and staggers from the room.

Iris in on the path outside the wall of the Institution. Caligari comes down the path towards camera, lurching from side to side and still clasping his precious book to his chest. (Still on page 84) He pauses and waves his hand wildly in the air, before turning back and staggering a little way down the path in the direction from which he has come. Then he turns again and walks back stiffly, turkey-toed. Suddenly a line of white writing appears on the Institution wall: 'DU MUSST CALIGARI WERDEN.' Caligari stops dead. He lurches towards the writing, which promptly disappears as he stretches out his hand to touch it. Shocked, he leaps

93

back on to the path. As he turns away from the wall the word 'CALIGARI' appears in enormous letters above his head. 'DU MUSST' appears again on the wall and 'CALIGARI' is written twice in the branches of the bramble which stands next to the wall. The words disappear and reappear with confusing rapidity, ending again with the sentence, 'DU MUSST CALIGARI WERDEN', written in the air at Caligari's side. At the sight of this last apparition, Caligari turns and flees down the path and disappears from sight.

Iris in on Francis and the doctors of the Institution still reading the diary. They look up and stare blankly at one another, stunned by what they have just read. Francis looks up and begins to speak.

While Francis and the three doctors are conferring behind the Director's desk, a man dressed as a peasant, with boots and cap, enters from the right. He respectfully removes his cap as he enters and then marches quickly up to the desk and gestures towards the left. What he says makes Francis rise swiftly up to his feet.

TITLE : '*We have found the sleep-walker out in the fields.*'

The peasant talks quickly for a moment to the four men behind the desk, then turns and leaves the office. Francis comes out from behind the desk and leads the three doctors after the man. Iris out. Iris in on a hillside scene, with the gaunt silhouette of a tree on the left. A group of men are standing over Cesare's prostrate body. The peasant we have just seen at the Institution joins the group, followed immediately by Francis, who darts forward and bends down to examine Cesare's body. After a careful examination, he rises slowly to his feet, lost in thought. Then he turns to the other members and indicates that he has finished with the body and that they can remove it. The men hoist Cesare on to their shoulders and follow Francis away down the hillside.

Francis enters the hall outside the Director's office, followed by four attendants bearing Cesare's body on a stretcher. Behind them come the three doctors in long white coats. Francis halts by the door to the office and signals to the attendants to put down the body. He opens the office door, pauses a moment, removes his hat and enters.

94

Inside the office Caligari is standing back to camera, his hands folded behind him. Francis walks towards the desk and stands waiting for Caligari to turn round.

As Caligari turns towards camera he seems to glare more intently than ever through his round spectacles. He is very heavily made up, with a broad white line over each brow. The wall behind him is covered with angular Cubist designs.

Francis stands facing Caligari as the latter completes his turn towards camera.

TITLE : ' *Mr. Director! Drop your pose. You are Caligari.*'

Caligari glares evilly at Francis.

Francis turns from the desk and calls to the men waiting outside to bring in Cesare's body. The men set the body down on the floor and then move to positions on both sides of the office. Caligari is framed between the two groups of men as he stands at his desk, aghast at the sight of the black-draped body in front of him, to which Francis points triumphantly. Caligari walks slowly forward with his stiff, turkey-toed gait. Francis looks at him accusingly and then springs forward and whips the cloth back from the face of the dead Cesare. Caligari staggers towards the body, spreading his arms to signify his grief, and collapses over it. (Still on page 101) There is a pause before Caligari slowly, terribly, rises to his feet again, glowering murderously at the group of doctors and attendants. This, we sense, is the lull before the storm. He hurls himself furiously at the older doctor's throat; the attendants manage to drag him back, but then he frees himself and leaps again at the doctor. Again the attendants manage to overpower and drag him back. An attendant rushes in with a straitjacket which he succeeds in passing over Caligari's head and shoulders while he is restrained by the other attendants. (Still on page 101) Finally Caligari is forced out of the room and Francis follows, his right arm extended above his head.

Caligari, straitjacketed, is dragged into a cell by four attendants. The cell is seen through an archway in a wall painted with light and dark patches; there are two high windows in the rear wall of the cell, which is painted with amoeboid shapes. In spite of his straitjacket, Caligari is still managing to put up a considerable struggle with his attendants. He sinks to his knees and forces the four men to drag him through the arch to the back of the cell, where they push him down on to a bunk bed. When they have succeeded in getting him into a sitting position, the four attendants leave the cell as two doctors enter and walk over to look at Caligari writhing on the bed. Francis follows them into the cell.

We see the face and shoulders of Caligari as he writhes impotently in the grip of the straitjacket; he is mouthing horribly as he becomes progressively more and more exhausted.

The doctors leave the cell and close a great triangular door behind them which swings shut slowly and inexorably, entirely fitting the archway which leads into the cell. Francis is left standing by the wall outside the door, very bewildered.

Iris in on Francis and the older man sitting on a bench by a wall, as in the opening scene of the film. Francis leans confidentially towards his companion and speaks to him.

TITLE : ' *And since that day the madman has never left his cell.*'

Francis looks down thoughtfully. The older man looks blankly in front of him, then makes as though to rise, drawing his cloak tightly about him. He finally rises completely and starts to move off, inviting Francis to come with him. Francis gets up from the bench slowly and the two men walk away down the path.

Jane, wearing a flowing white gown, is sitting on the left of the courtyard of the Institution, which looks exactly as it did during the previous sequences : radial lines painted on the ground and the arched facade to the rear. Now, however, numbers of people are moving about randomly and among a group sitting in the leather armchairs on the right of the courtyard we recognise the dark slim figure of Cesare, in the act of rising from his chair. (Production still on page 102)

Jane, her long black hair surmounted by a tiara, sits absolutely immobile; her lips are slightly pursed.

A woman in black enters the courtyard and curtsies respectfully to Jane, who turns her head towards her in brief acknowledgement. Cesare slowly wanders over from right; he is holding a white

96

flower, the petals of which he is gently stroking.

An old man with a mane of white hair and a thick beard orates and gesticulates; he is dressed in a pin-stripe suit with a bright watch chain across his middle.

The face of the old man, as he shouts dramatically, is creased with deep lines; his eyes are almost Mongoloid.

The old man continues his passionate oration, waving his right arm up and down dramatically.

In the meantime, Cesare, still engrossed in examining his flower, has moved nearer camera. A man dressed in black scuttles furtively left to right across the yard.

In one of the large leather armchairs, a woman in her late thirties, wearing very heavy eye make-up, is playing an imaginary piano, her arms stretched out in front of her.

Meanwhile, the woman in black has concluded her bow to Jane and Cesare has turned away from camera. The older doctor — the one attacked by Caligari — talks to a well-dressed young lady in the centre of the courtyard, before turning and leaving. Francis and his older companion enter right.

Suddenly Francis notices Cesare — leaning against the wall of the courtyard behind the chairs and still engrossed in his flower — and recoils, falling backwards against his friend.

Cesare's face looks sad and melancholy as he gazes tenderly at his flower; his hair is now tidily brushed back from his brow.

Francis recovers his balance and pulls his companion away from Cesare; he points towards the latter across the older man and whispers urgently. Francis's expression throughout this exchange is wild and staring; he is not at all the bright, intense young man of former scenes.

TITLE : ' Look! There is Cesare. Never ask him to tell your fortune; it will mean death for you.'

Francis continues to confide in the older man who has turned to stare at Cesare.

Cesare, gaunt and melancholy, continues his examination of the flower, supporting the bloom with his hand.

The older man stares in astonishment at Francis, then backs away, alarmed, and hurries from the courtyard. Francis, shoulders bowed, remains, a hang-dog expression on his face. Suddenly, however, his face breaks into a childish grin as he sees someone off left. He stretches his arms in front of him and totters towards whoever he has seen.

Francis comes up to Jane, who is still sitting down and staring blankly in front of her; as he approaches her, his childish grin intensifies. He advances on her with his arms outspread as though about to clasp her in a passionate embrace. She, however, shows absolutely no response to his advances and Francis is obliged to content himself with gripping the back of her chair, from which position he speaks passionately to her.

TITLE : ' *Jane! I love you. Won't you ever marry me?* '

Francis pleads with the girl.

His passionate entreaties elicit little response from Jane, who, bored and condescending, turns her head slowly away from him.

TITLE : ' *We queens — we may never choose as our hearts dictate.*'

The girl slowly turns her head back again until she is facing camera, staring blankly ahead.

Francis looks deeply hurt as he draws back from Jane's chair. The girl freezes into immobility and Francis turns to face the rear of the courtyard.

The inmates of the Institution are still milling about the courtyard; in one corner, near the facade of the building at the rear of the courtyard, two young women are deep in argument. Francis, moving away from Jane's chair, suddenly notices something under one of the arches which causes him to lurch wildly across the yard to get a better view of what he has seen, before dashing towards the arches.

The Director of the Institution, a neat, benevolent-looking man, walks down the steps and under the arch into the courtyard. He is meticulously dressed in a frock-coat, waistcoat and light-coloured trousers. His face bears a very vague resemblance to Caligari's.

The Director enters the courtyard through the centre arch. Francis, meanwhile, stands with the two young women who have been arguing. They are restraining him from advancing closer to the Director.

The Director's face bears a kindly smile.

The Director stops for a moment to talk to the bearded old man who has previously been seen delivering a speech to an imaginary audience. Francis is still being restrained by the two young women. The Director leaves the old man and walks forward into the court-yard, hands still folded behind his back. Francis jerks himself free from the restraining hands of the two young women.

Francis screams something out through clenched teeth. The two women on either side of him draw back, their hands raised in fear. (Still on page 102)

TITLE: *'You all believe I am mad. That is not true. It is the Director who is mad.'*

Francis clenches his fists above his head, screams and lurches for-ward.

The Director is continuing his walk forward, oblivious that Francis is rushing towards him from behind. Francis grasps hold of the Director's shoulders, shouting loudly.

TITLE: *' He is Caligari, Caligari, Caligari.'*

A furious struggle develops in the courtyard. The older doctor rushes in to the Director's aid, while another attendant comes from another side of the courtyard and grabs Francis round the waist. The two women who have held Francis look on with extreme alarm.

Francis is surrounded by a crowd of attendants, one of whom is brandishing a straitjacket. They succeed in subduing him and slip the straitjacket over him, bundling him away out of the courtyard. (Still on page 103)

Francis is dragged into the same cell in which Caligari was earlier incarcerated. (Still on page 103) The group of attendants around Francis is followed into the cell by the Director and two white-coated doctors, who bend inquisitively over Francis after he has been deposited on the bunk bed at the back of the cell. The atten-dants leave the Director with Francis.

Francis is now half-sitting on the bed as the three men bend over him. (Still on page 104) The Director straightens up and turns towards camera, fumbling in the inside pocket of his frock coat from which he produces a pair of round spectacles. He slowly pulls the spectacles over his ears, giving him an extraordinary resemblance to Caligari. Francis, seeing this, stares at the Director like a terrified child. The Director, however, takes his head gently in both hands and lays it on the pillow. He turns towards camera, thoughtfully removes his glasses and speaks.

TITLE : ' *At last I understand the nature of his madness. He thinks I am that mystic Caligari. Now I see how he can be brought back to sanity again.*'

The Director turns slightly right, brushes back a few stray wisps of hair, and, looking well-pleased with himself, replaces his spectacles in his coat pocket. Iris out on the Director's face, a thoughtful, pleased expression on it.
Fade in.

TITLE : *THE END*.

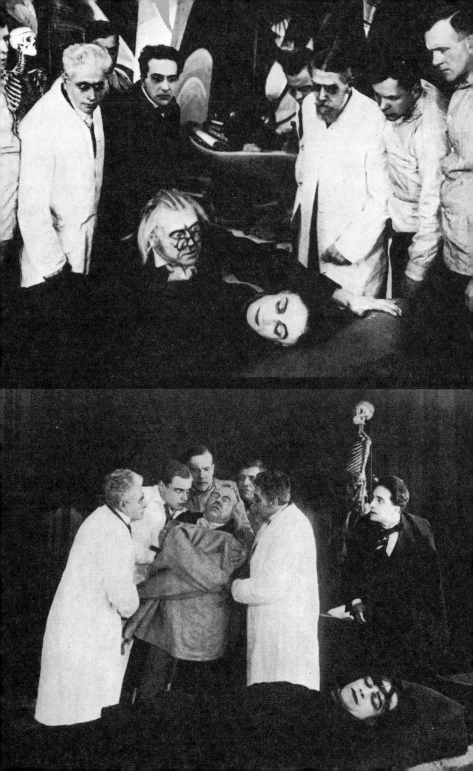

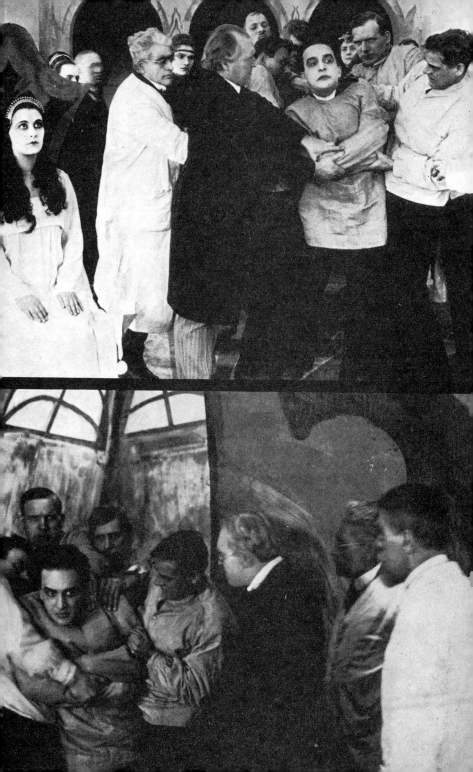

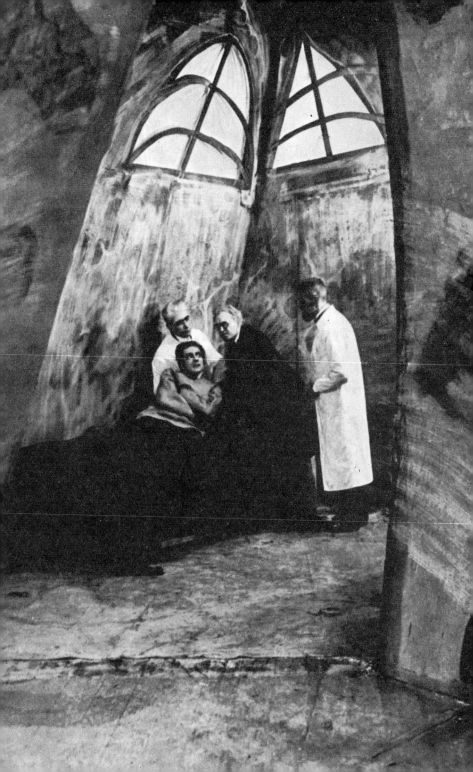